OUR NIG

or, Sketches from the Life of a Free Black,
In a Two-Story White House, North
Showing that Slavery's Shadows Fall Even There
By "Our Nig"

HARRIET E. WILSON

The first published African American woman's novel

Edited, with an introduction and notes, by R J Ellis

TRENT EDITIONS

Published by Trent Editions 1998
Reprinted 1999, 2001

Trent Editions
Department of English and Media Studies
The Nottingham Trent University
Clifton Lane
Nottingham NG11 8NS

Introduction © R J Ellis

Printed in Great Britain by Goaters Limited, Nottingham
ISBN 0 905 48884 9

Contents

Introduction

In May 1982 the eminent critic Henry Louis Gates Jr demonstrated that Harriet E. Wilson's autobiographical novel *Our Nig* was written by an African American woman living in Milford, New Hampshire during the decades leading up to the Civil War.[1] It is hard to overstate the significance of this moment, or of Gates's subsequent publication of a facsimile edition of *Our Nig* in 1983, since the novel is now generally accepted to be the first African American novel written by a woman and the first African American novel published in the USA. For a number of obvious reasons Alice Walker seemed in 1983 the best person to bear testimony to the significance of the book's re-publication. 'I sat up most of the night pondering the enormous significance of Harriet Wilson's *Our Nig*' – these words of Walker's appeared on the cover of the second paperback facsimile edition (also published in 1983).

Her words ring as true today as they did then. As recently as 1985 Barbara Christian can be found suggesting that Frances Ellen Watkins Harper's 1892 novel, *Iola LeRoy: Shadows Uplifted*, is 'considered by many to be the first ... by an Afro-American woman to be published';[2] now, by 1998, *Our Nig* has fully supplanted it. This revision represents a leap back in time of one third of a century: the first African American woman's novel now dates not from 1892, long after Abraham Lincoln's Emancipation Proclamation, but from 1859, when slavery still existed in the Southern United States and the 1850 Fugitive Slave Law held sway, allowing slaves to be recaptured, even in US States where slavery had been abolished.

This chronological alteration in itself would be of 'enormous significance' (what would or could be the equivalent for Anglo-Saxon women's writing, I wonder?). But far more has happened, for Wilson's novel is also one that raises and explores dilemmas enduringly central to African American women's writing.

Our Nig's Basic Plot

Frado (short for Alfrado, also named as 'Our Nig') is deserted when a young child by her white mother after the death of her African American father. She is abandoned in the home of the Bellmonts, where she becomes an indentured servant and is treated cruelly – both by her white mistress, Mrs Bellmont and by Mary Bellmont, her daughter. The males in the Bellmont household seek to protect Frado, by and large ineffectually, but she finally learns to stand up for herself. When eighteen, and come of age, she leaves, meets up with a young African American posing as a runaway slave, marries, has a child and is deserted by him. She experiences acute poverty and poor health (the latter precipitated by the years of abuse she has suffered). These lead to her being forcibly separated from her child. In parallel with the unfolding of Frado's story, the novel pays some attention to the lives of the Bellmonts, and the trials they too go through because of the harsh materialism of Mrs Bellmont.

In this introduction I want to explore in some detail how several of the themes that emerge in this straightforward story are taken up by Wilson: the problem of 'naming' (– how African Americans can assume cultural identities); the problem of subsistence – both economic and socio-cultural; and the human experience of enduring pain. Over-archingly, there is also the problem, one facing all African American writers, of how to discover a workable genre within which to explore these and other dilemmas encountered by African Americans in the United States – a process recurrently leading women writers into a complex series of debts and borrowings (intertextual exchanges), resulting in the creation of writing residing in no single literary genre (novel, autobiography, documentary, popular fiction), but bridging between several different genres.

Harriet Wilson and African American Writing

A tempting starting point when approaching these issues is to note that, also in 1983, the very year in which she lauded Gates and Wilson, Alice Walker won the Pulitzer Prize for her novel, *The Color Purple*.

In its opening pages Walker's novel, itself an intertextual experiment with genre, portrays the plight of a young African American girl who, separated from her children, becomes, effectively, the enslaved servant of a man, Mr. _____ (his name being one small indication of *The Color Purple*'s exploration of the problem of naming). Mr. _____ beats Celie, reduces her to bare subsistence and abuses her cruelly.[3] In portraying such abuse, Walker's novel, over a century after slavery was abolished, plainly has ironic affinities with slave narratives written before the Civil War. In some ways, however, *The Color Purple*'s affinities with *Our Nig* are even more compelling. The two texts are, of course, not symmetrical, since Walker's protagonist, Celie, lives in the post-Bellum segregated South whilst Frado in *Our Nig* lives in the ante-Bellum, 'free' North. However, both Celie and Frado, despite being emancipated, are in a very real sense enslaved: just like Celie, Frado is beaten, abused cruelly and eventually separated from her child. Indeed, in the introduction to *Our Nig*, in the book's final chapter and in its closing pages, Wilson defines as her key motive for writing the book an attempt to get her child back by earning sufficient money to reclaim him from charitable support.

These suggestive parallels between Wilson's novel and *The Color Purple* could bear further elaboration, and provide one seductive way of illuminating the reason for the 'enormous significance' of *Our Nig*. I write 'seductive' because, by the narrowest of chronological margins, *The Color Purple* simply cannot be indebted to *Our Nig*. Plainly, though, both draw on a core set of concerns that African American women writers recurrently address when treating with the multiple ways in which Black women are oppressed by 'the tripartite crossfire of masculine prejudice, white illogical hate and Black lack of power.'[4]

Our Nig's Historical Co-ordinates

Both *The Color Purple* and *Our Nig*, then, articulate the ways in which race, sex and class combine to constitute an oppressive whole very much greater than its constituent parts. Yet these potentially close comparisons exist despite the fact that *The Color Purple* is a historical novel dealing with the life of its protagonist from (roughly) the middle of the 1890s to the middle of the 1940s,[5] whilst *Our Nig* portrays the life of its young protagonist from the early 1840s to the late 1850s. Celie's and Frado's lives are thus separated by half-a-century, by the American Civil War and geographically by the Mason-Dixon line, yet close congruences exist between them. This in itself directs our attention forcibly to the distinctly unfree position of 'free' African Americans in the ante-Bellum North, and how their position and plight establish historical patterns which are to be replicated in post-Bellum America, after the abolition of slavery nationwide. Drawing parallels between Frado, an ante-Bellum Northern African American, and Celie, an oppressed female Black in the segregationist post-Bellum South, is one way of understanding why Gates is tempted to identify Wilson as 'a fugitive slave from Virginia' – a speculation we now know to be improbable.[6]

Plainly, the position of African Americans in the ante-Bellum North, as the very existence of the Fugitive Slave Laws indicates, was, in important respects, just as beleaguered as that of their Southern counterparts, both before and after the Civil War. But beyond these (ultimately limited) generalisations, there is need to establish some historical specificity, to map out the precise co-ordinates framing Frado's oppression. The Fugitive Slave Laws, particularly the one passed in 1850, bear eloquent testimony concerning how *close* to slavery African Americans in the Northern States were at that time, since these laws allowed unscrupulous slave hunters to try to capture any African American they encountered in the North, simply by representing them as escaped slaves. This common experience of racist persecution and oppression was particularly true for female 'free' African Americans in the North, who were especially valued for their reproductive potential and so especially vulnerable to 'recapture'. *Our Nig* offers to its readers one of the very few narrative treatments by African American women of these ante-Bellum modes of oppression in the North of the United States, 'watched by kidnappers' and surrounded by 'traps' (pp. 69-70). That Wilson's text was also fiction gave her a particular licence to dramatise these patterns and draw them into sharp focus. Thus, though Wilson is dealing with what Jean Fagan Yellin describes as one element of the 'standard pattern' of African American narratives when writing of Northern racial discrimination, she brings a new and powerful narrative agency to bear on this inflammatory historical problem.[7]

We can thus identify *Our Nig* as a significant intervention: Alice Walker described it as 'a whole new layer of time and existence'. A 'whole new layer', indeed: between 1810 and 1850 the free Black population in America had increased fourfold in size.[8] Such studies as that of the historian Leonard P. Curry show conclusively that Wilson's portrait of the position of the free Black in the Northern States possesses considerable accuracy. Like Wilson, in her individual portrait of the plight of Frado, Curry shows the lot of 'free' Northern Blacks to be complexly proscribed by racial discrimination: in terms of employment, education and religion, and, more generally, in cultural terms. Perhaps most significantly, in certain key respects, such discrimination was exercised more pronouncedly in the North than in the South (though the South, of course, more than made up for this by preserving the institution of slavery). This shows up above all in employment: 'there was no lack of racial prejudice in the South, but it does not appear that this prejudice made itself felt in the form of discrimination in employment to the degree that was common in the northern cities'.[9] Wilson's portrait of Frado's struggles to find employment after she comes of age and leaves the Bellmonts is thus symptomatic.

The perspective of *Our Nig* upon this Northern matrix of racism and discrimination is that of a female African American indentured serving-girl. To call her book an exploration of a 'two-story' house, as Wilson does in her subtitle, is thus entirely appropriate. Frado lives in *Single*ton, but double-standards plainly operate in the town. Frado suffers horribly at the hands of the Bellmont family for whom, as a child, she works. The portrait of what might be described as 'domestic peonage' becomes a powerful general indictment of African American oppression in the ante-Bellum 'free' North, especially when we remember that domestic service was at that time the predominant employment for free Blacks, and particularly free Black women.[10] The growing amount of research that has been done on Harriet Wilson's life adds weight to the potency of this critique, because it suggests that *Our Nig*'s narrative offers a fair degree of authenticity, closely matching its author's actual experiences. Henry Louis Gates Jr and his colleagues, at first, and subsequently Barbara A. White,[11] undertook extensive research into the community records of Milford, New Hampshire, where Gates deduced that Mrs H. E. Wilson had resided when undergoing the experiences she records.

Our Nig's Autobiographical Co-ordinates

The research of Gates and White needed to be careful, since Wilson had published her book anonymously as *Our Nig* by "Our Nig". Discovering the identity of the author involved following up two clear clues in the text: firstly the fact that Wilson had copyrighted the book in her own name; secondly the mention of the town of Milford in one of the testimonials appended to the novel. Bringing these two facts together and then carrying out a great deal of painstaking archival research enabled Gates (and his colleagues) and then White to piece together the story. What follows is a brief account of Gates's and White's combined findings. (Research into Wilson's life and circumstances will surely continue.)

Harriet Wilson seems to have been born in the 1820s (most probably between 1824 and 1828; Gates proposes 1827 or 1828, White is in more doubt). Just possibly she was born in Virginia, but it is more likely she was born in New Hampshire. Her maiden name was Adams. Harriet Adams-Wilson spent her childhood serving as an indentured servant until the age of eighteen for the Nehemiah Haywards, a farming family living on the edge of Milford (White made this discovery; Gates mistakenly believed she worked for another Milford family, that of Samuel Boyles). Nehemiah Hayward had inherited his farm from his parents, who had set it up, with its orchards, sheep flocks, and a river flowing through it. He had a sister, Sally Hayward, who owned a 'right' in the farmhouse and lived in part of it. The Haywards were a moderately well-off but not wealthy family. Sometime in the 1830s, probably the early thirties, Harriet Adams-Wilson had joined the household as a 'free colored person'.[12] White speculates that most probably Harriet Adams-Wilson was 'bound out' to the Haywards,[13] who therefore were paid to look after her.

All of this matches up closely with incidents in Wilson's narrative in *Our Nig*. But, beside their stewardship of Harriet Wilson, other events in the lives of the Haywards have been uncovered, and these in turn correspond with events depicted in *Our Nig*. To give a few examples: the youngest daughter, Rebecca Hayward, died in her teens on a visit to Baltimore; another daughter, Lucretia Hayward, married a man from Vermont and went out 'West'; George Hayward, the eldest son, went to Baltimore to work, eventually returning home to Milford, ill, with his wife and child, and then dying. All these facts more or less match up with incidents in *Our Nig*. In turn, about the time when the evidence suggests that Adams-Wilson would have completed her indenturement and left the Haywards, the name Adams and later Wilson occur in the details of Milford's expenditures on the poor and in the records of the County Farm. These appearances in charity records again correspond well with the account in *Our Nig* of Frado's departure from the Bellmonts, aged eighteen, and her subsequent impoverishment. The accompanying testimonials at the end of *Our Nig* further underline these parallels. In particular the name change (Adams to Wilson) indicates that Adams-Wilson did indeed get married, directly replicating Frado's unfortunate match. Furthermore, evidence suggests that Wilson, like Frado, did move to Massachusetts (Boston), later returning to Milford. Finally, Mrs Hayward does seem to have removed to Baltimore late in her life, just as Mrs Bellmont does in the text. In all these ways the life of 'Our Nig', the young African American woman called Frado, consistently runs in close parallel with the probable life of Harriet Adams-Wilson in the Hayward household.

However, the novel also offers a few other details that as yet cannot be found in the historical record. Some relate to Frado's mother, Mag, about whom nothing is known. The core subject of *Our Nig* also cannot be found in the historical records, by its very nature. This is found in the long central section, which focuses on Frado's maltreatment at the hands both of Mrs B., described as a 'she-devil', and, to a lesser extent, at the hands of her daughter, Mary. This sadistic story of private mistreatment, of course, lies outside of the public archive, as does the failure of the Bellmont males to intervene, despite their professed sympathy and liking for Frado. Given the date of publication of the novel, just prior to the Civil War, there are very substantial ironies in the Bellmonts' maltreatment of Frado. Indeed, it is difficult to draw back from a symbolic reading, within which Frado's lot becomes representative of female African Americans' general, barely documented 'enslavement' in the ante-Bellum United States. What we have in *Our Nig* is a history that goes beyond or, rather, goes *inside* the historical records.

Our Nig as Autobiography

Because of this close correspondence between *Our Nig*'s representation of the Bellmonts and Frado and details about the Haywards and Wilson in the historical records, it is easy to suggest the book is best read as an autobiography. There are a few disparities: Barbara White notes that *Our Nig* makes a few significant adjustments to the facts as found in the archival records. But these differences, apart from a simplification of the Hayward family tree, boil down by and large to questions of relatively minor chronological incongruences and to how the novel alters more or less peripheral incidents. In both cases, when all is said and done, it can be argued that both written records and people's memories can be vague about such details.

Regarding the work as principally autobiographical, then, is perfectly tenable, and this approach gains further validation from two facts. Firstly, it was to be Gates and not Wilson who defined the narrative as a novel. As White points out, Wilson offered no definite description of how she herself regarded her work beyond that found in the subtitle, which refers to 'sketches';[14] furthermore, one of the testimonials at the end, far from regarding the book as fiction, actually calls it an 'autobiography' (p. 75). Secondly, we must notice the use of the first person in the first three chapters' titles ('Mag Smith, My Mother'; 'My Father's Death', 'A New Home for Me'). This use of the first-person pronoun ('my', 'me') could suggest that because Harriet Wilson's narrative so closely adheres to the details of her own life she had no consciousness of her narrator as a fictional persona. Alternatively these chapter-titles could suggest that Wilson either set out initially to write a first-person autobiography and then, changing her approach, edited slightly carelessly, or wanted to give Frado a personal voice through the device of using first-person chapter headings.

Adopting this view – of the text as autobiography – proves fruitful. We can now take on board the idea that writing autobiography can be regarded as a means of writing oneself into greater self-awareness: a process of self-realisation through self-representation – a winning of self-consciousness.[15] This self-creation can be seen to be of singularly pronounced importance to female African Americans, who have systematically, through processes of oppression, been denied full access to a sense of self as an actor and self-author – to a sense of subjectivity.[16] Thus, one typically discovers in African American autobiographical narratives what amounts to moments of sudden and profound insight (epiphanies), which gain sharpened definition by the very process of being 'written'. In Richard Wright's autobiography, *Black Boy* (1945) there is Richard's graduation speech, which performs precisely this sort of function. Richard's moment of epiphany at his high school is in turn intertextually echoed in *I Know Why the Caged Bird Sings*, where Maya Angelou sets up a series of gender-inflected ironic contrasts between the dilemmas confronting her autobiographical self and those confronting Wright's 'Richard', as Maya prepares for her own graduation.[17] Both are enlightened inwardly when faced with their schools' graduation addresses, but in Maya's case this hinges on the socially precarious location of African American woman's triply marginalised identity – delimiting the problems of agency that beset and confront her.

This is also a central problem for Frado. Oppressed, beaten and abused, she can hardly ever act for herself or gain self-expression in the Bellmont household under the eye of the ironically labelled 'Mrs. B.' and her daughter. Only outside of the house, during her shepherding duties (when she plays her dangerous trick on a ram – whose male sex is surely significant), or by climbing onto the roof of the house, or when attending school for the few years that this is allowed, can she give vent to the 'exuberance of spirit almost beyond restraint' described in Chapter II.

Frado's central moment of epiphany comes not at school, however, but later, when, after years of abuse, in Chapter X, she finally stands up to Mrs. B. at the woodpile:

> ... Mrs. B. ... followed her, and, snatching from the pile a stick, raised it over her:
>
> "Stop", shouted Frado, "strike me and I'll never work a mite more for you;" and throwing down what she had gathered, stood like one who feels the stirring of free and independent thoughts.
>
> By this unexpected demonstration, her mistress, in amazement, dropped her weapon, desisting from her purpose of chastisement. ... Frado ... did not know, before, that she had a power to ward off assaults. (pp. 56-57)

Unsurprisingly, this moment of self-realisation for Frado is also one in which she assumes agency as an acting subject, walking off towards the house whilst 'her mistress follow[ed] with the wood she herself was sent after'.

Our Nig as a Realist Novel

However, more complex things happen at the woodpile than just a simple process of autobiographical self-realisation. This is clearly and unambiguously marked in the text by the use of a third-person narrative, setting up a dialectic between the consciousness of Frado ('know[ing] ... she had the power to ward off assaults') and the intervention of the voice of the narrator: 'she ... stood *like* one who feels the stirring of free and independent thoughts' (p. 56; my italics).

It is in fact difficult to weigh the precise impact of the use of the word 'like' in this passage. For the critic Elizabeth Breau, this shows that Frado here still lacks a fully internalised consciousness, only *appearing* this way.[18] Alternatively it could be proposed that Frado for the first time senses that she can indeed have some right to be an acting agent. Or maybe, in a more sophisticated way, she adopts what she knows to be a conventional 'dramatic pose' (the melodramatic pose appropriate to the imaginary stage direction: 'she felt the stirrings of free and independent thought', to be found in many contemporary popular prints and illustrations). By adopting this melodramatic pose Frado could communicate to Mrs. B. that the latter, for her own safety, was best advised to fall back, now that Frado has become a full-grown woman, almost of age. However we choose to read this episode, we are being required to insert some interpretive mediation between the narrative and the conventions of 'frank autobiography'. What exactly Wilson means is not overt or fully interpreted for us as readers.

We can, therefore, when discussing *Our Nig*, choose to foreground instead the text's deployment of a third-person narrative voice: in the woodpile incident, it functions as a mediating voice, problematising the issue of agency (who can act and who cannot) in a complex way. It is just not possible simply to read *Our Nig* as autobiography, and even when reading it as an autobiographical novel we are forced to note again its persistent departures from accuracy, as revealed by the researches of Barbara A. White. When the text's large-scale pruning of the size of the Bellmont/Hayward family, its adjustments to the course of that family's history and its chronological alterations are placed alongside its employment of a third-person narration, these features can all combine to act as powerful endorsements for Gates's contention that the book should be first identified as a novel.

Considered as a novel, it has then to be identified as a narrative in fact offering a deal of prose verisimilitude:

There was, on their way home, a field intersected by a stream over which a single plank was placed for a crossing. It occurred to Mary that it would be a punishment to Nig to compel her to cross over; so she dragged her to the edge, and told her authoritatively to go over. Nig hesitated, resisted. Mary placed herself behind the child, and, in the struggle to force her over, lost her footing and plunged into the stream. Some of the larger scholars being in sight, ran, and thus prevented Mary from drowning and Frado from falling. Nig scampered home fast as possible, and Mary went to the nearest house, dripping, to procure a change of garments. She came loitering home, half crying, exclaiming, "Nig pushed me into the stream!" She then related the particulars. Nig was called from the kitchen. Mary stood with anger flashing in her eyes. Mr. Bellmont sat quietly reading his paper. He had witnessed too many of Miss Mary's outbreaks to be startled. Mrs. Bellmont interrogated Nig.

"I didn't do it! I didn't do it!" answered Nig, passionately, and then related the occurrence truthfully.

The discrepancy greatly enraged Mrs. Bellmont. With loud accusations and angry gestures she approached the child. Turning to her husband, she asked,

"Will you sit still, there, and hear that black nigger call Mary a liar?"

"How do we know but she has told the truth? I shall not punish her," he replied ... . (p. 16)

The tone here is predominantly one appropriate to a verisimilitudinous documentary report, but in fact there are a series of movements from part to whole (metonymic slides) generated within the story, widening the significance of these simple events: Mary's decision to make Frado risk a ducking links up with many other incidents in Frado's oppression. Indeed, Frado's resistance to and her resulting struggle with and victory over Mary foreshadow the final 'woodpile' victory over Mrs. B., the central matriarch, who she finally faces out in Chapter X. The aggressive use of the word "'nigger'" by Mrs. B. as she defends Mary after her ducking, glosses the ironic use of the word 'Nig' in the title of the book, illuminating the venom parcelled within what might otherwise be held to be 'merely' a term of endearment ('our nig') that the Bellmonts use to refer to Frado. All this is plainly novelistic, and draws the text into some sort of relationship with the conventions of the realist novel. Indeed, the work as a whole spends a considerable amount of narrative energy building up an accurate picture of Frado's daily labours and mistreatments in the Bellmont household. Thus the contexts are established for Frado's final, total debilitation and the need for her to write the book to earn a living. In this line, Frado's dog, Fido can be seen as a 'brilliant ... motif,' to use Barbara A. White's phrase,[19] dialectically commenting on the life of Frado in the Bellmont household. The incident where Frado gets Fido to lick the plate used by Mrs. B. before she herself will use it is full of recursive ironies concerning Frado's position in the household and her politicised appreciation of these realities: made to re-use a dirty plate she deliberately inserts a dog's life between her's and Mrs. B.'s. Each regards the other as lower than a dog – though Frado it is who, emblematically, almost has the dog's name, Fido.

Relatedly, a key context that the text indicates thematically is the socio-economic. The position of African Americans in the US has recurrently required clear economic reference for its proper illumination, be it chattel slavery in the South or wage slavery in the North. Plainly, for Wilson, an African American living in the post-slavery North but in ante-Bellum America, economics was, first and last, of crucial significance: the dollar sign resonates throughout her text, from the Bellmonts' constant evaluations of Frado's worth at the start to Frado's own impoverishment at the end. Barbara A. White has explored this motif ably.[20] I would wish here to stress the way in which, within the text, the economics places Frado in a form of enslavement – her domestic peonage under the Bellmonts. She must, the text constantly reminds us, earn her keep: "'I'll beat the money out of her if I can't get her worth any other way,'" says Mrs. B. in Chapter VIII. Cost and worth are matters of constant debate in connection with Frado, and this motif becomes noticeably more pronounced as the story progresses.

With hindsight, deep ironies pertaining to the position of African

Americans in the US after the end of the Civil War can be detected in the lot of Frado as a 'Free Black' in the post-Abolition North. Nationwide, abolition was to introduce new modes of African American servitude: debt-peonage in the agrarian South and the continuation of racist discrimination in the urban North by way of 'wage slavery.' In both cases these oppressions were buttressed by ideological practices, defined by segregation in the South and ghettoisation in the North. Frado's truncated education, and the Northern whites' debates about whether it should occur at all generates (even to the present day) potent resonances. Recurrently, the treatment of Frado, one of the few African American narrative portraits of the fate of 'free Blacks' in ante-Bellum America, foreshadows the besetting problems of inequality that remain unresolved, despite the repeated use of legislative adjustments to the status of African Americans, beginning with Lincoln's Emancipation Proclamation of 1862. Lincoln's Proclamation comes only three years after Wilson's novel was published, and it is surely worth reminding ourselves that *Our Nig* was published barely two years before the Civil War commenced. It is quite openly dealing with what was the burning issue of the time, the position of African Americans in US society, and its metonymic slides convey us into the very heart of the nexus of issues investing the problem of servitude and the position of the African American.

In particular we are lead inexorably to confront the issue of racism. The failure of anyone to intervene in an enduring and effective fashion on Frado's behalf during the years of mistreatment that she suffered is recurrently revealed to be rooted firmly in racist assumptions. For example, she is instructed by Mr Bellmont in Chapter X that she must endure the beatings she deserves and only avoid the ones she was "'*sure*'" she did not; furthermore, this instruction is given her after the onset of the debilitating and enduring illness caused by her previous mistreatment, that has left her too ill to continue to endure her vicious mishandling. In this way Mr. Bellmont's statement becomes one legitimating not only ante-Bellum slavery but also endemic racism: African Americans, he *naturally* assumes, will from time to time deserve a beating. Racism's hegemonic grip could not be more economically illuminated.

Our Nig and Sentimentalism

This question of the role of racism, as opposed simply to that of slavery, in the processes of oppressing African Americans, was in fact of considerable topical interest at that time. The simplest way of suggesting this is by pointing to the way in which the issue is debated in Harriet Beecher Stowe's enormously successful *Uncle Tom's Cabin, or, Life Amongst the Lowly*. In this book a point at issue is the precise attitude of the forty-five year old Miss Ophelia to African Americans. Her prejudices come under textual scrutiny during her visit to her cousin's Louisiana estate. We are told in Chapter XV (in an irony that begs for close analysis) that Ophelia is 'the absolute bond-slave of the "ought" ... . Her standard of right was so high, so all-embracing, so minute, and making so few concessions to human frailty, that, though she strove with heroic ardour to reach it, she never actually did so'.[21] Stowe's irony is far-reaching and carefully contrived here, for it later becomes quite crucial to one sub-plot of her story that this minutely scrupulous female cannot readily bring herself to be touched by black skin:

> "I've always had a prejudice against negroes," said Miss Ophelia, "and it's a fact, I never could bear to have that child [Topsy] touch me; but I don't think she knew it."
>
> "Trust any child to find that out," said St. Clare; "... all the substantial favours you can do them, will never excite one emotion of gratitude whilst that feeling of repugnance remains in the heart ... ."[22]

Needless to say, the example of Little Eva, particularly her death-bed reaching out to Topsy, enables Miss Ophelia to conquer her racist aversion, and as a consequence to succeed Eva as Topsy's mentor:

> "*She* [Eva] said she *loved* me," said Topsy – "she did! Oh dear! Oh dear! there ain't *nobody* left now – there ain't!" ...

"Topsy, you poor child," she [Miss Ophelia] said, as she led her into her room, "don't give up! *I* can love you, though I am not like that dear little child. I hope I've learnt something of the love of Christ from her. I can love you; I do, and I'll try to help you to grow up a good Christian girl."

Miss Ophelia's voice was more than her words, and more than that were the honest tears that fell down her face. From that hour she acquired an influence over the mind of the destitute child that she never lost.[23]

The 'honest tears' here mark the end of Ophelia's hypocrisy. One could argue that in *Our Nig*, in contrast, no-one in the Bellmont household manages to bring themselves to this pitch. Thus Frado is in fact left in destitution by the whole family – and, indeed, by almost the whole New England community.

Quite plainly, in considering *Our Nig*'s relation to these portrayals of Northern racism, I have moved on to consider another sub-genre of the novel in relation to Wilson's text, and in the process have implicitly begun to question the adequacy of identifying *Our Nig* as either autobiography or realistic writing (or, even, as an amalgam of both). Though there are recurrent passages of straightforward prose description in *Our Nig*, there are also, interlaced amongst them, contrasting passages which derive from other generic identities, rooted in more popular manifestations of the novel genre: the sentimental and the sensational. Parts of *Our Nig* clearly derive from what was, in the 1830s and 1840s, a recurrent hybrid that draws symbiotically on these two popular traditions, a hybridity which *Uncle Tom's Cabin* typifies well enough.

The points that I have just made about *Uncle Tom's Cabin* in fact owe a substantial debt to the analysis of that novel made by Jane Tompkins, in her *Sensational Designs*, and I find her argument in that book again pertinent when turning to a consideration of *Our Nig*'s relationship to the sentimental and sensational.[24] Tompkins suggests that the deployment of sensation and sentiment in the popular fiction genre that Nina Baym labelled 'woman's fiction' and Mary Kelley as the 'domestic novel' is strategic.[25] It roots itself in its readers' established familiarity with the way the genre sets up conventional expectations about the deployment of certain plot and character patterns. Tompkins views these deployments as 'designs', *designed* to move the audience, through the emotions they arouse: in the case of *Our Nig*, to move them to a re-consideration of their beliefs about 'free' Northern blacks. The sensational representation of Frado's suffering and the sentimental introduction of a series of hackneyed love-and-marriage and death-bed sub-plots are designed to draw on the strategies of those *designedly* popular novels (self-)consciously seeking to advance radical programs within well-established popular generic conventions.

Frado's sensational sufferings therefore, interlaced as they are with soft-focus explorations of the Bellmonts' domestic travails, establish a moving series of contrasts, which provide a measure of the Northern family's ultimate heartlessness. This process is made all the more potent by the way the narrative's dynamic relegates those incidents that conventionally would be positioned as centrally important (New England family love problems) to the margins of the story's concerns, where they become, more than anything else, only further illustrations of white America's potential for cruelty, evidenced by its racism and rooted in its material greed. Thus Mrs. B. opposes the marriage of Jack and Jenny on monetary grounds, paralleling a key motive in her maltreatment of Frado. This is indeed a *moving* critique, but it also operates more complexly, as an intertextual exposé of the actual ideological softness at the core of white abolitionist writing. For example, Stowe textually legitimates Miss Ophelia's conversion by way of Eva's saintly example ('a child shall lead them') and therefore leaves untouched the other strand that her book lays bare but which Wilson strips naked: the economic buttressing that always already invests the moral argument. Thus the child Frado, far from leading (as she might in a sentimental plot), is repeatedly reduced to being led (as she is 'led' into hatred by her resistance), and Mary, the story's other central child, is one of these leaders – both in mistreating Frado and in calculating her worth. Where

Eva leads Topsy to the love of Christ, Mary (and Mrs. B., behind and before her) leads Frado to a state of mind where her developing conversion to Christianity seems to come to an unresolvable hiatus upon Mary's death. Frado cannot help but celebrate Mary's passing in a quite unchristian way:

> "She got into the river again, Aunt Abby, didn't she; the Jordan is a big one to tumble into, any how. S'posen she goes to hell, she'll be as black as I am. Wouldn't mistress be mad to see her a nigger!" and others of a similar stamp, not at all acceptable to the pious, sympathetic dame. (p. 57)

I write 'seems to come to a hiatus' here because the text, perhaps necessarily, does not explicitly represent this 'termination', instead allowing the matter of Frado's religious conversion indecisively to trail away in the text, instead of reaching a conventional climax. This omission lends weight to the contention that the text is best read as a novel, since the testimonials at the end show that Wilson herself had a good knowledge of the Bible.

My working assumption here (unfortunately an unprovable one as we will probably never know significantly much more about Wilson than we do at present) is that Wilson had read Stowe. We can safely say that Wilson was well-read (the quotations introducing each chapter are unfailingly apposite) and that she had some familiarity with the popular novel genre – her deployment of sentimental and sensation fiction's language, imagery and plot-devices all point to this. We can also say that one likely source for this was *Uncle Tom's Cabin*, given its familiarity to Northern audiences. Where, exactly, Wilson would have read Stowe's 1852 novel could now lead on to yet one further level of speculation. Wilson's long convalescences provide a sustained series of opportunities for reading, of course. But I have only ventured into this line of speculation about Wilson's reading so that I can make make the point that a plausible place where she could have found a copy of

Stowe is, surprisingly, the 'Two-*Story* White House, North' of the Haywards, had she returned there in 1852 (as she just may have done).

Our Nig and Abolitionist Slave-Narratives

Barbara A. White has uncovered compelling evidence that the Haywards had, at the very least, strong abolitionist connections and, quite probably, counted themselves as an abolitionist family.[26] This leads White to speculate that when Wilson states in her preface that she has 'purposely omitted what would most provoke shame in our good anti-slavery friends at home' she is obliquely alluding to the fact that she has 'purposely' arranged her text so that Frado omits to refer to any abolitionist sympathies on the halves of the Bellmonts. This speculation seems to me more sensible than the suggestion of Cynthia J. Davis that what Frado is concealing to spare the feelings of 'good anti-slavery friends' is a rape, at the hands of a Northern white.[27] Rather, White focuses on the sudden outburst of Frado near the end of her narrative concerning '... professed abolitionists who didn't want slaves at the South, nor niggers in their own houses, North'. White views this as a demonstration of the way in which Frado's experiences at the hands of the abolitionist connected Haywards have created a deep-rooted mistrust of the motives and conduct of abolitionists generally, and aided her in discovering the recurrent existence of hypocrisy in their ranks. I myself would endorse all this, by noting that we know that Milford was a town that professed strong abolitionist sympathies (Gates notes the formation in Milford of the 'come-outers' in December 1842, a group of prominent citizens who held meetings encouraging waverers to 'come out' as abolitionists).[28] However, I would also emphasise two other things about Wilson's decision not to 'provoke shame in our good anti-slavery friends'.

Firstly, the way this issue is taken up late in the novel suggests further, and quite different, intertextual resonances with Stowe's work. Wilson truly lays bare the obstructive problem of racist hypocrisy in the progress of white and African American relations, most sophisticatedly by the insertion of the deadly word, 'professed', alluding as it does to the problem, in the North in the late 1840s, of being sure, if Black, of who exactly one's friends were, as the dominant ideological mood swung towards abolitionism in some areas (as the activities of the Milford 'come outers' suggest). In this atmosphere one's 'convictions' came to be not the only plausible motive when taking up the abolitionist cause. After all, there *was* money in it, as Frado's eventual husband proves when faking fugitive slave status to exploit the abolitionist lecture circuit. Of course this dilemma – the need to weigh motives – becomes far more complex under the offensive impact of the Fugitive Slave Laws, which allowed slave bounty-hunters to recapture runaways anywhere and punished those who impeded their recapture. In the period 1850 to 1860 a test was set for anti-slavery white Americans when faced with a fugitive on the one hand and the law of the land on the other – a test within which consistency, conviction and commitment, and not mere verbal professions, would become materially crucial. After all, real monetary reward could flow from recanting on one's abolitionist principles.

Secondly, I would want to stress that the real power of Wilson's text lies in leaving this issue open-ended in her text. We are told by Wilson in her preface that she has suppressed certain facts to avoid provoking shame in 'our good anti-slavery friends', but what *facts*, exactly, are being omitted in *Our Nig* to spare their ('our') feelings? And are we supposed to read the adjective 'good' ironically? We are invited to speculate disturbingly, as the text unfolds. The novel lays down the proposition that many abolitionists were in fact racist and/or hypocritical. We are left to think through the multiple possible consequences.

The sentence in the preface about not provoking 'shame' amongst 'anti-slavery friends' also draws attention to the text's relationship to the burning issue of the day: the status of slavery as a legal entity. Black writing, as an act of agency in the ante-Bellum United States, sets up an inevitable dialectic with the progress of abolition and the issue of emancipation. As a consequence, African American writing in this period was dominated by texts directly addressing these subjects:

the potent 'slave narrative' genre which has been much analysed. Since these texts, within their formulaic construction, drew on the conventions of sentimental and sensation novels, it can be reasonably posited that Wilson grew familiar with these conventions whilst reading slave narratives. The point here is that, in important regards, *Our Nig* adheres to the formulae of the slave narrative. To seize on the most obvious and most central example, Frado's moment of epiphany, when at the woodpile she realises the potential she has for agency, maps precisely onto the conventional structure of the slave narrative. We can therefore twin Frado's cry and the narrator's comment, "'Stop ... strike me and I'll never work a mite more for you;" [she said and] ... stood like one who feels the stirring of free and independent thoughts', with Frederick Douglass' epiphany in his *Narrative*:

> I resolved to fight, and suiting my action to this resolution, I seized Covey hard by the throat ... . For the whole six months afterwards that I spent with Mr. Covey, he never laid the weight of his finger upon me in anger. ...
>
> This battle with Covey was the turning-point in my career as a slave ... He can only understand the deep satisfaction which I experienced, who has himself repelled by force the bloody arm of slavery. I felt as I have never felt before. It was a glorious resurrection from the tomb of slavery, to the heaven of freedom. ... I now resolved that, however long I might remain a slave in form, the day had passed forever when I could be a slave in fact.[29]

The characteristic use of chiasmus by Douglass here links back to his introduction to his battle with Covey: 'You have seen how a man was made a slave; you shall see how a slave was made a man'.[30]

As with Harriet Beecher Stowe, it is tempting now to suggest that a conscious intertextuality exists. In key respects, Wilson's novel offers a rebuttal of Douglass' claim that only those who had experienced 'the bloody arm of slavery' and then repelled it 'by force' could 'understand' Douglass' 'deep satisfaction'. Frado's satisfaction is also surely 'deep', as she returns to the house ahead of Mrs. B. after her woodpile showdown. Even more subtly, Wilson revises the formulation of Douglass' climactic assertion: 'slave' > 'man'. Her book shows how a girl made into a servant makes herself into a woman, in a revision that underlines how female African Americans are positioned differently in the processes of racist exploitation, a position which also reveals the clear masculinist traces in Douglass' account of African American rebellion.

Our Nig and Racism

In the process of exploring *Our Nig*'s shifting generic identity we have in a sense gone full circle: by now comparing *Our Nig* to autobiographical slave narratives we have almost returned all the way back to considering *Our Nig* as autobiographical, since the extent to which the text can be considered a slave narrative is plainly circumscribed by Wilson's actual status: one of emancipated female servility. This re-positions her within the processes of African American representation and self-representation in a complex manner. Crucial to an understanding of this is the exploitative relationship struck up with her by a man passing himself off as a 'free Black', whom she marries. He emerges as a charlatan who deserts her. Whilst she bears a child, he voyages abroad, offering 'humbugs for hungry abolitionists'.

This extraordinary revelation of African American mendacity needs to be carefully weighed. On the one hand, of course, Frado's husband's exploitation of abolitionist generosity can be seen as an act of justifiable retaliation, given the persistence of abolitionists' demeanings of African Americans, either through offensive patronage (the abolitionist advice offered to Douglass, that he should restrict himself to 'the facts' of his 'story' is a pertinent and infamous example of this),[31] or through the disabling, hypocritical persistence of racism. Here Stowe's representation of Miss Ophelia's prejudiced aversion to touching Blacks is given a new and potent twist by Wilson: 'Faugh! to lodge one, to eat with one; to admit one through the front door; to sit next one; awful!' (pp. 69-70).

This provides us with the simplest way of understanding what it is that Wilson means when in her preface she says that she wishes to spare the feelings of her 'good anti-slavery friends'. In fact, one can read this remark with the deepest irony. Little 'shame' can have been left unprovoked amongst her 'good anti-slavery friends' in these crisp denunciations of 'professed abolitionists' and, more generally, Northern whites' hypocritical and unchristian behaviour.

This is perhaps most centrally marked by the persistent deviations from the conventions of the different genres upon which *Our Nig* draws. In particular, Wilson's refusal to deploy the conventional domestic sentimentalism investing (white) women when portraying the violent sadism of Mrs. B. and Mary is not consistent at all with a desire to avoid provoking 'shame'. White women are being wrested from their generic location, and this, crucially, is in line with some commentators' suggestions that some Northern white women were the most viciously racist.[32] The nascent sentimental novel is further aborted by the failure to deliver in full any final message of Christian consolation, which seems instead to be tacked on rudimentarily, as Frado depends on a charitableness that has repeatedly failed in the past. (A final irony here is that we know Wilson's son in fact died shortly after the novel was published, in February 1860.)

Just as the novel deviates from sentimental models, so the use of the third person establishes an ironic distance between Wilson and her autobiographical persona, Frado, who should stand in the text as the conventional (albeit re-positioned) slave-narrative protagonist. In this respect, the use of testimonials urging on the reader both the worthiness and honesty of the author and the authenticity of the narrative demands particular pause. This was, after all, a convention of the slave narrative (for example, both Frederick Douglass, in his *Narrative*, and Harriet A. Jacobs, in her *Incidents in the Life of a Slave Girl, Written by Herself*, employ this device).[33] That Wilson uses the device herself is one further indication of her knowledge of slave narratives. But, untypically, Wilson's testimonial writers are not identifiable figures. Indeed, Elizabeth Breau suggests that the authenticity of the testimonials is dubious, and, quite possibly, that their actual author was Wilson herself.[34] Breau thus diverges from Gates, who saw the testimonials as supporting a view of the novel as autobiographically-centred. Breau, in disagreeing, actually quotes Gates himself to support her argument: the initials 'C. D. S.', used by one of Wilson's testifiers, were at that time the legal abbreviation for 'Colored Indentured Servant',[35] which may suggest that the writer of this tribute to Wilson was actually Wilson herself. I am in this respect therefore inclined to side with Breau, since the style of both the preface (signed by Wilson) and the testimonials display some congruences.[36] We may never know for sure who is in the right in this regard. Indeed, I may prove to be wrong in siding with Breau. But I am inclined this way on sentimental grounds as well as evidential ones.

Let me explain why. Readers of *Our Nig* cannot help but notice how Wilson in her preface pitches her appeal for assistance to her 'colored brethren universally', who, it seems, she expects to be her 'public'. I suggest two things hold true of this audience. Firstly, they would be familiar with the slave narrative, and the framing established by the authorial 'preface' and final testimonials immediately echoes this genre. Secondly, they would be very likely to pick up on the complex ironies embedded in the text concerning the precarious, marginalised position of 'Free Blacks' in the North. Yet, simultaneously, Wilson would need to be leery: there is a real risk of bringing down on herself white opprobrium. The text was surely going to be read by whites (as the testimony of 'Margaretta Thorn' indicates) and so she ran the risk of being identified, despite using a pseudonym. This was particularly worrying, since whites must for her remain important benefactors and continue to constitute a key 'market-share' for her needlework and other products. The shuttle between autobiographical realism and fictional sentimentalism now becomes highly motivated, a means of simultaneously advancing and then refracting a fully frank revelation of the recurrent realities of African American domestic servitude on the one hand, and the ramifications of racism on the other. Just consider the slipperiness of Wilson's twin narrative comments: that the white American Mag had 'descended another step down the ladder of infamy' through her marriage to the African American Jim and that Jim was 'proud of his treasure – a white wife'; 'He thought of the pleasing contrast between her fair face and his own dark skin' (p. 4). The intersection of racism, sexuality and their ideological representation, and of a contingent political economy, is encapsulated stunningly in this double-edged portrait and its ironic commentary.

The balance is precarious indeed, as is the way in which Nig's embrace of Christianity seems to be unsure and incomplete. Here again the appended testimonials shore up the text, by constantly offering the reassurance of good Christian sentiment. The text is in a sense rescued, pulled back to stand on familiar ground by these conventional framings. Thus, the assertion that Frado is writing the book to raise money to rescue her son from poverty falls wholly within slave narrative conventions: Noah Davis earlier that year, had published in Baltimore his narrative stressing that self-same motivation.² But even in this case an ironic difference continues: Frado seeks to rescue her son not from slavery but from Northern white charity – a damning commentary.

Our Nig demands an extraordinary alertness from its readers as it sustains these complex negotiations. This complexity stems from a desperate need to keep the narrative balanced on its knife-edge, as Wilson always already had been balanced during her life. This is revealed nowhere more sharply than in the portrait of Frado, come of age and having left the Bellmonts, quite literally running the gauntlet of not only racist 'professed abolitionists' but also, we are specifically told, slave-hunting 'kidnappers'. The Fugitive Slave Laws here cast their long and deadly shadow across the text, alongside those of ideologically-embedded racism, reminding us forcibly how important it is to use inverted commas round the adjective 'free' when depicting the position of African Americans in the ante-Bellum North.

Language, signs and meanings are always of great importance to Frado, whether these are the unstated terms of indenturement binding her to the Bellmonts, the laws governing the positions of slaves and runaways, or the racist discourses that legitimate these practices. Harriet Wilson, significantly, problematises language in her very title, *Our Nig* by "Our Nig". The inverted commas that constantly invest African Americans' lives literally invest Frado's representation, to the extent that the conventions of 'entitling' are fractured. As Gates has noted, the use of inverted commas here is plainly ironic,[38] and I agree: *Our Nig by "Our Nig"* is indeed a *mis*titling. But this irony is multi-levelled. One question raised, quite explicitly, is: can we identify to whom exactly the 'we' refers on the title page: who exactly is regarding Frado as "Our Nig". In the main title, *Our Nig*, '*Our*' possibly refers to the Bellmonts, who (after all) coin the nickname – indicating that they somehow believe they own Frado, that she is '*their* Nig'. But, even granted this, who does the second "Our" denominate, in the pseudonym "Our Nig"? Just as the noun cannot now refer only to Frado, since it also refers to the text's author, so the pronoun cannot be limited to the Bellmonts, but rather enjoys a wider reference. It is, in a real sense, chosen and employed by 'us': 'We' do the naming – the North of the United States, where Frado exists, but also society more broadly still. She is in this sense '*our* Nig'. Racism and its ramifications are thus forcibly brought home to all Americans and, indeed, to 'us' all, to whom *Our Nig by "Our Nig"* speaks down the decades.

I should finally and all too briefly like to offer a few acknowledgments and thanks: to the scholars who have previously worked on Wilson and whose work has proved so valuable to me, particularly Henry Louis Gates Jr and Barbara H. White; to my colleague and friend, John Lucas, to Helen Doodson, Kerry Secker and Carmen Templeton; to Mary Dawson and Celia Coates of the Nottingham Trent University Library; to John Oldfield, for his cover design; to Carolyn R. Fawcett of Harvard College Library; to the Reverend Neil Dixon; and most of all, first and last, to Maggie Ellis.

R J Ellis

Footnotes.

1. See Henry Louis Gates Jr, 'Introduction' to Harriet E. Wilson, *Our Nig* (New York: Random House, 1983), pp. xi-lv; Henry Louis Gates Jr, 'Parallel Discursive Universes: Fictions of Self in Harriet E. Wilson's *Our Nig*', in Henry Louis Gates Jr, *Figures in Black: Words, Signs and the Racial Self* (New York: Oxford University Press, 1987), pp. 125-149.

2. Barbara Christian, 'Shadows Uplifted', in Judith Newton and Deborah Rosenfelt, eds., *Feminist Criticism and Social Change* (London: Methuen, 1985), p. 181.

3. Alice Walker, *The Color Purple* (London: The Women's Press, 1983), pp. 3ff.

4. Maya Angelou, *I Know Why the Caged Bird Sings* (1968; rpt. London: Virago Press, 1984), p. 265. This formulation is recurrently advanced: '... although we may already know about racial oppression, sexual oppression, class oppression, we may not know how ... these modes are interrelated.' – Susan Willis, 'Black Women Writers', in Gayle Greene and Coppélia Kahn, *Making a Difference* (London: Methuen, 1985), p. 212. It remains commonplace. See, for example, Sedgwick's comment that 'every issue of racial meaning must be embodied through the specificity of a particular class position – and every issue of class ... through the specificity of a particular gender position ... and vice versa': Eve Kosofsky Sedgwick, *Epistemology of the Closet* (London: Harvester, 1991), p. 31.

5. The chronology of *The Color Purple* is not wholly clear, but can be deduced with some precision. See R. J. Ellis, 'Out from Under the Cucumber: *The Color Purple*'s Discursive Critique of Postmodern Deferral', in Theo D'haen and Hans Bertens, eds., *Liminal Postmodernisms* (Amsterdam: Rodopi, 1994), pp. 287-288.

6. Henry Louis Gates Jr, 'Notes to the Text', in Harriet E. Wilson, *Our Nig* (New York: Random House, 1983), p. x; Barbara H. White, '"Our Nig" and the She Devil: New Information about Harriet Wilson and the "Bellmont" Family', *American Literature* Vol. 65, No. 1, p. 26.

7. Jean Fagan Yellin, *The Intricate Knot* (New York: New York University Press, 1972), p. 126.

8. J. B. DeBow, quoted in Leonard B. Curry, *The Free Black in Urban America 1800-1850* (Chicago: The University of Chicago Press, 1981), p. 6.

9. Curry, p. 34.

10. Curry, pp. 22ff.

11. Gates, 'Introduction', passim; David A. Curtis, 'Chronology', in Gates, ed., *Our Nig*, pp. xiii-xxvii; David Ames Curtis and Henry Louis Gates Jr, 'Establishing the Identity of the Author of *Our Nig*', in Joanne M. Braxton and Andrée Nicola McLaughlin, *Wild Women in the Whirlwind* (New Brunswick: Rutgers University Press, 1990), pp. 48-69; White, "Our Nig", pp. 19-45.

12. White, p. 42.

13. White, p. 47.

14. White, pp. 41ff.

15. See, for an example of this line of argument, Stephen Butterfield, *Black Autobiography in America* (Boston: Massachusetts University Press), p. 3 and passim.

16. See, for example, Patricia Waugh, *Feminine Fictions: Revisiting the Postmodern* (London: Routledge, 1989), pp. 2-16.

17. Wright, *Black Boy* (1945; rpt. London: Pan Books, 1988), pp. 199ff.; Angelou, *I Know Why the Caged Bird Sings*, pp. 177ff.

18. Elizabeth Breau, 'Identifying Satire: *Our Nig*', *Callaloo* Vol. 16, Prt. 2 (1993), p. 464.

19. White, "Our Nig", p. 22.

20. White, "Our Nig", pp. 33ff.

21. Harriet Beecher Stowe, *Uncle Tom's Cabin, or, Life Amongst the Lowly* (1852; rpt. Harmondsworth: Penguin, 1981), p. 248.

22. Stowe, *Uncle Tom*, p. 410.

23. Stowe, p. 432.

24. Jane Tompkins, *Sensational Designs: The Cultural Work of American Fiction, 1790-1860* (New York: Oxford University Press, 1985), passim.

25. Nina Baym, *Woman's Fiction: A Guide to Novels by and about Women in America*, 1820-1870 (Ithaca: Cornell University Press, 1978), pp. 29ff; Mary Kelley, P*rivate Women, Public Stage: Literary Domesticity in Nineteenth Century America* (Oxford: Oxford University Press, 1984), p. 14ff.

26. White, "Our Nig", p. 34ff.

27. Cynthia J. Davis, 'Speaking the Body's Pain: Harriet Wilson's *Our Nig*', *African American Review* Vol. 27, No. 3, p. 397.

28 Gates, 'Notes to the Text', in Gates, ed., *Our Nig*, p. v.

29. Frederick Douglass, *Narrative of the Life of Frederick Douglass, an American Slave, Written by Himself* (1845; rpt. Harmondsworth: Penguin, 1982), p. 113.

30. Douglass, *Narrative*, p. 107.

31. Frederick Douglass, *My Bondage and My Freedom* (1855; rpt., ed. William L. Andrews, Urbana: University of Illinois Press, 1987), p. 220.

32. '... the feeling was more bitter in women than in men ... and in the north than in the south' (Edward S. Abdy, in Curry, *The Free Black*, p. 83). See also Brenda E. Stevenson, *Life in Black and White: Family and Community in the Slave South* (New York: Oxford University Press, 1996).

33. Douglass, *Narrative*, pp. 33-43; Harriet A. Jacobs, 'Appendix', *Incidents in the Life of a Slave Girl* (1861; rpt., ed. Jean Fagan Yellin, Cambridge, Mass.: Harvard University Press, 1987), pp. 203-5.

34. Breau, 'Identifying Satire', p. 458.

35. See Henry Louis Gates, Jr., 'Notes to the Text', in Gates, ed., *Our Nig*, p. x.

36. A few examples of these congruences: Allida: 'he left ... and embarked for sea' (p. 134), Wilson: 'He left her ... – embarked at sea' (p. 127); Margaretta Thorn: 'I hope those who will call themselves friends of our dark-skinned brethren, will lend a helping hand' (p. 140), Wilson: 'I sincerely appeal to my colored brethren universally for patronage, hoping they will not condemn this attempt ...' (p. 3); C. D. S.: 'I hope no one will refuse to aid her in her

work, as she is worthy the sympathy of all Christians' (p. 140), Wilson: 'Reposing on God ... Still an invalid, she asks your sympathy, gentle reader ... Enough has been unrolled to demand your sympathy and aid' (p. 130).

37. Noah Davis, *A narrative of the life of Rev. Noah Davis, a colored man* (Baltimore: J. F. Weishampel, 1859).

38. Gates, 'Introduction', in Gates, ed., *Our Nig*, p. xxvii.

Suggestions for Further Reading

Braxton, Joanne M. & Andrée Nicola McLaughlin (1990). *Wild Women in the Whirlwind: Afra-American Culture and the Contemporary Literary Renaissance*. New Brunswick: Rutgers University Press.

Carby, Hazel (1987). *Reconstructing Womanhood: the Emergence of the Afro-American Woman Novelist*. Oxford: Oxford University Press.

Curry, Leonard B. (1981). *The Free Black in Urban America 1800-1850*. Chicago: The University of Chicago Press.

Davis, Cynthia J. (1993). 'Speaking the Body's Pain: Harriet Wilson's *Our Nig*', *African American Review* 27:3, 391-404.

Doriani, Beth Maclay (1991). 'Black Womanhood in Nineteenth Century America: Subversion and Self-Construction in Two Women's Autobiographies', *American Quarterly* 43:2, 199-222.

Elkins, Stanley (1959). *Slavery: A Problem in American Institutional Life*. Chicago: University of Chicago Press.

Foreman (1990). 'The Spoken and the Silenced in *Incidents in the Life of a Slave Girl* and *Our Nig*', *Callaloo: Journal of African American Arts and Letters*, 13:2, 313-324.

Foster, Frances Smith (1993). *Written by Herself: Literary Production by African American Women, 1746-1892*. Bloomington: Indiana State University Press.

Gardner, Eric (1993). '"This Attempt of Their Sister": Harriet Wilson's *Our Nig* from Printer to Readers', *New England Quarterly*, Vol. 66 No. 2 (June), 226-246.

Gates, Henry Louis Jr. (1987). *Figures in Black: Words, Signs and the Racial Self*. Oxford: Oxford University Press.

Gates, Henry Louis Jr. (1993). 'Wilson, Harriet E.', in D. C. Hine, E. B. Brown and R. Terborg-Penn, eds., *Black Women in America: An Historical Encyclopedia,* Vol. II. Bloomington: Indiana University Press.

Harris, Susan K. (1990). *Nineteenth Century American Women Novelists: Interpretative Strategies.* Cambridge: Cambridge University Press.

Jackson, Blyden (1989). *A History of Afro-American Literature: The Long Beginning, 1746-1895.* Baton Rouge: Louisiana University Press.

Matthews, Geraldine O. (1975). *Black American Writers, 1773-1949.* Boston: G. K. Hall.

Tate, Claudia (1990). 'Allegories of Black Female Desire; or, Rereading Nineteenth-Century Sentimental Narratives of Black Authority', in Cheryl A. Wall, ed., *Changing Our Own Words: Essays on Criticism, Theory and Writing by Black Women.* London: Routledge, 98-126.

Tompkins, Jane (1985). *Sensational Designs: The Cultural Work of American Fiction, 1790-1860.* New York: Oxford University Press.

Weld, Theodore Dwight and Angelina Grimké (1839). *American Slavery As It Is: Testimony of a Thousand Witnesses.* New York: American Anti Slavery Society.

White, Barbara A. (1993). '"Our Nig" and the She-Devil: New Information about Harriet Wilson and the "Bellmont" Family', *American Literature* 65:1, 19-52.

Wilson, Harriet (1859). *Our Nig.* Rpt., ed. with an introduction by Henry Louis Gates Jr. New York: Vintage Books, 1983.

A Note on the Text

This is a modern edition of *Our Nig.* Accordingly, some minor changes have been made to the original text, printed by Geo. C. Rand and Avery in Boston in 1859. This first edition was printed slightly carelessly, and the changes carried out are aimed to make the novel read more easily. As these changes are, nevertheless, not that numerous, the notes at the end of the text indicate where these minor alterations have been made. This text, however, does not aim to be a full variorum edition.

Facing page: a facsimile of the first edition's title page.

OUR NIG;

OR,

Sketches from the Life of a Free Black,

IN A TWO-STORY WHITE HOUSE, NORTH.

SHOWING THAT SLAVERY'S SHADOWS FALL EVEN THERE.

BY "OUR NIG."

"I know
That care has iron crowns for many brows;
That Calvaries are everywhere, whereon
Virtue is crucified, and nails and spears
Draw guiltless blood; that sorrow sits and drinks
At sweetest hearts, till all their life is dry;
That gentle spirits on the rack of pain
Grow faint or fierce, and pray and curse by turns;
That hell's temptations, clad in heavenly guise
And armed with might, lie evermore in wait
Along life's path, giving assault to all." — HOLLAND.

BOSTON:

PRINTED BY GEO. C. RAND & AVERY.

1859.

Preface

In offering to the public the following pages, the writer confesses her inability to minister to the refined and cultivated, the pleasure supplied by abler pens. It is not for such these crude narrations appear. Deserted by kindred, disabled by failing health, I am forced to some experiment which shall aid me in maintaining myself and child without extinguishing this feeble life. I would not from these motives even palliate slavery at the South, by disclosures of its appurtenances North. My mistress was wholly imbued with *southern* principles. I do not pretend to divulge every transaction in my own life, which the unprejudiced would declare unfavorable in comparison with treatment of legal bondmen; I have purposely omitted what would most provoke shame in our good anti-slavery friends at home.

My humble position and frank confession of errors will, I hope, shield me from severe criticism. Indeed, defects are so apparent it requires no skilful hand to expose them.

I sincerely appeal to my colored brethren universally for patronage,[1] hoping they will not condemn this attempt of their sister to be erudite, but rally around me a faithful band of supporters and defenders.

H. E. W.[2]

CHAPTER I

Mag Smith, My Mother[3]

Oh, Grief beyond all other griefs, when fate
First leaves the young heart lone and desolate
In the wide world, without that only tie
For which it loved to live or feared to die;
Lorn as the hung-up lute, that ne'er hath spoken
Since the sad day its master-chord was broken!

Moore[4]

Lonely Mag Smith! See her as she walks with downcast eyes and heavy heart. It was not always thus. She *had* a loving, trusting heart. Early deprived of parental guardianship, far removed from relatives, she was left to guide her tiny boat over life's surges alone and inexperienced. As she merged into womanhood, unprotected, uncherished, uncared for, there fell on her ear the music of love, awakening an intensity of emotion long dormant. It whispered of an elevation before unaspired to; of ease and plenty her simple heart had never dreamed of as hers. She knew the voice of her charmer, so ravishing, sounded far above her. It seemed like an angel's, alluring her upward and onward. She thought she could ascend to him and become an equal. She surrendered to him a priceless gem, which he proudly garnered as a trophy, with those of other victims, and left her to her fate. The world seemed full of hateful deceivers and crushing arrogance. Conscious that the great bond of union to her former companions was severed, that the disdain of others would be insupportable, she determined to leave the few friends she possessed, and seek an asylum among strangers. Her offspring came unwelcomed, and before its nativity numbered weeks, it passed from earth, ascending to a purer and better life.

"God be thanked," ejaculated Mag, as she saw its breathing cease; "no one can taunt *her* with my ruin."

Blessed release! may we all respond. How many pure, innocent children not only inherit a wicked heart of their own, claiming life-long scrutiny and restraint, but are heirs also of parental disgrace and calumny, from which only long years of patient endurance in paths of rectitude can disencumber them.

Mag's new home was soon contaminated by the publicity of her fall; she had a feeling of degradation oppressing her; but she resolved to be circumspect, and try to regain in a measure what she had lost. Then some foul tongue would jest of her shame, and averted looks and cold greetings disheartened her. She saw she could not bury in forgetfulness her misdeed, so she resolved to leave her home and seek another in the place she at first fled from.

Alas, how fearful are we to be first in extending a helping hand to those who stagger in the mires of infamy; to speak the first words of hope and warning to those emerging into the sunlight of morality! Who can tell what numbers, advancing just far enough to hear a cold welcome and join in the reserved converse of professed reformers, disappointed, disheartened, have chosen to dwell in unclean places, rather than encounter these "holier-than-thou" of the great brotherhood of man!

Such was Mag's experience; and disdaining to ask favor or friendship from a sneering world, she resolved to shut herself up in a hovel she had often passed in better days, and which she knew to be untenanted. She vowed to ask no favors of familiar faces; to die neglected and forgotten before she would be dependent on any. Removed from the village, she was seldom seen except as upon your introduction, gentle reader, with downcast visage, returning her work to her employer, and thus providing herself with the means of subsistence. In two years many hands craved the same avocation; foreigners who cheapened toil and clamored for a livelihood, competed with her, and she could not thus sustain herself. She was now above no drudgery. Occasionally old acquaintances called to be favored with help of some kind, which she was glad to bestow for the sake of the money it would bring her; but the association with them was such a painful reminder of by-gones, she returned to her hut morose and revengeful, refusing all offers of a better home than she possessed. Thus she lived for years, hugging her wrongs, but making no effort to escape. She had never known plenty, scarcely competency; but the present was beyond comparison with those innocent years when the coronet of virtue was hers.

Every year her melancholy increased, her means diminished. At last no one seemed to notice her, save a kind-hearted African, who often called to inquire after her health and to see if she needed any fuel, he having the responsibility of furnishing that article, and she in return mending or making garments.

"How much you earn dis week, Mag?" asked he one Saturday evening.

"Little enough, Jim. Two or three days without any dinner. I washed for the Reeds, and did a small job for Mrs. Bellmont; that's all. I shall starve soon, unless I can get more to do. Folks seem as afraid to come here as if they expected to get some awful disease. I don't believe there is a person in the world but would be glad to have me dead and out of the way."

"No, no, Mag! don't talk so. You shan't starve so long as I have barrels to hoop. Peter Greene boards me cheap. I'll help you, if nobody else will."

A tear stood in Mag's faded eye. "I'm glad," she said, with a softer tone than before, "if there is *one* who isn't glad to see me suffer. I b'lieve all Singleton wants to see me punished, and feel as if they could tell when I've been punished long enough. It's a long day ahead they'll set it, I reckon."

After the usual supply of fuel was prepared, Jim returned home. Full of pity for Mag, he set about devising measures for her relief. "By golly!" said he to himself one day – for he had become so absorbed in Mag's interest that he had fallen into a habit of musing aloud – "By

3

she'd *marry* me."

shouted Pete Greene, suddenly starting from an unobserved
the rude shop.

ere you come from, you sly nigger!" exclaimed Jim.

ome, tell me, who is't?" said Pete; "Mag Smith, you want to
marry?"

"Git out, Pete! and when you come in dis shop again, let a nigger
know it. Don't steal in like a thief."

Pity and love know little severance. One attends the other. Jim
acknowledged the presence of the former, and his efforts in Mag's
behalf told also of a finer principle.

This sudden expedient which he had unintentionally disclosed, roused
his thinking and inventive powers to study upon the best method of
introducing the subject to Mag.

He belted his barrels, with many a scheme revolving in his mind,
none of which quite satisfied him, or seemed, on the whole, expedient.
He thought of the pleasing contrast between her fair face and his own
dark skin; the smooth, straight hair, which he had once, in expression
of pity, kindly stroked on her now wrinkled but once fair brow. There
was a tempest gathering in his heart, and at last, to ease his pent-up
passion, he exclaimed aloud, "By golly!" Recollecting his former
exposure, he glanced around to see if Pete was in hearing again. Satisfied
on this point, he continued: "She'd be as much of a prize to me as
she'd fall short of coming up to the mark with white folks.
I don't care for past things. I've done things 'fore now I's 'shamed of.
She's good enough for me, any how."

One more glance about the premises to be sure Pete was away.

The next Saturday night brought Jim to the hovel again. The cold
was fast coming to tarry its apportioned time. Mag was nearly despairing
of meeting its rigor.

"How's the wood, Mag?" asked Jim.

"All gone; and no more to cut, any how," was the reply.

"Too bad!" Jim said. His truthful reply would have been, I'm glad.

"Anything to eat in the house?" continued he.

"No," replied Mag.

"Too bad!" again, orally, with the same *inward* gratulation as before.

"Well, Mag," said Jim, after a short pause, "you's down low enough. I don't see but I've got to take care of ye. 'Sposin' we marry!"

Mag raised her eyes, full of amazement, and uttered a sonorous "What?"

Jim felt abashed for a moment. He knew well what were her objections.

"You's had trial of white folks, any how. They run off and left ye, and now none of 'em come near ye to see if you's dead or alive. I's black outside, I know, but I's got a white heart inside. Which you rather have, a black heart in a white skin, or a white heart in a black one?"

"Oh, dear!" sighed Mag; "Nobody on earth cares for *me —*"

"I do," interrupted Jim.

"I can do but two things," said she, "beg my living, or get it from you."

"Take me, Mag. I can give you a better home than this, and not let you suffer so."

He prevailed; they married. You can philosophize, gentle reader, upon the impropriety of such unions, and preach dozens of sermons on the evils of amalgamation. Want is a more powerful philosopher and preacher. Poor Mag. She has sundered another bond which held her to her fellows. She has descended another step down the ladder of infamy.

CHAPTER II

My Father's Death

Misery! we have known each other,
Like a sister and a brother,
Living in the same lone home
Many years — we must live some
Hours or ages yet to come.

Shelley [5]

Jim, proud of his treasure, – a white wife, – tried hard to fulfil his promises; and furnished her with a more comfortable dwelling, diet, and apparel. It was comparatively a comfortable winter she passed after her marriage. When Jim could work, all went on well. Industrious, and fond of Mag, he was determined she should not regret her union to him. Time levied an additional charge upon him, in the form of two pretty mulattos, whose infantile pranks amply repaid the additional toil. A few years, and a severe cough and pain in his side compelled him to be an idler for weeks together, and Mag had thus a reminder of by-gones. She cared for him only as a means to subserve her own comfort; yet she nursed him faithfully and true to marriage vows till death released her. He became the victim of consumption. He loved Mag to the last. So long as life continued, he stifled his sensibility to pain, and toiled for her sustenance long after he was able to do so.

A few expressive wishes for her welfare; a hope of better days for her; an anxiety lest they should not all go to the "good place;" brief advice about their children; a hope expressed that Mag would not be neglected as she used to be; the manifestation of Christian patience;

these were *all* the legacy of miserable Mag. A feeling of cold desolation came over her, as she turned from the grave of one who had been truly faithful to her.

She was now expelled from companionship with white people; this last step – her union with a black – was the climax of repulsion.

Seth Shipley, a partner in Jim's business, wished her to remain in her present home; but she declined, and returned to her hovel again, with obstacles threefold more insurmountable than before. Seth accompanied her, giving her a weekly allowance which furnished most of the food necessary for the four inmates. After a time, work failed; their means were reduced.

How Mag toiled and suffered, yielding to fits of desperation, bursts of anger, and uttering curses too fearful to repeat. When both were supplied with work, they prospered; if idle, they were hungry together. In this way their interests became united; they planned for the future together. Mag had lived an outcast for years. She had ceased to feel the gushings of penitence; she had crushed the sharp agonies of an awakened conscience. She had no longings for a purer heart, a better life. Far easier to descend lower. She entered the darkness of perpetual infamy. She asked not the rite of civilization or Christianity. Her will made her the wife of Seth. Soon followed scenes familiar and trying.

"It's no use," said Seth one day; "we must give the children away, and try to get work in some other place."

"Who'll take the black devils?" snarled Mag.

"They're none of mine," said Seth; "what you growling about?"

"Nobody will want any thing of mine, or yours either," she replied.

"We'll make 'em, p'r'aps," he said. "There's Frado's six years old, and pretty, if she is yours, and white folks'll say so. She'd be a prize somewhere," he continued, tipping his chair back against the wall, and placing his feet upon the rounds, as if he had much more to say when in the right position.

Frado, as they called one of Mag's children, was a beautiful mulatto,[6] with long, curly black hair, and handsome, roguish eyes, sparkling with an exuberance of spirit almost beyond restraint.

Hearing her name mentioned, she looked up from her play, to see what Seth had to say of her.

"Wouldn't the Bellmonts take her?" asked Seth.

"Bellmonts?" shouted Mag. "His wife is a right she-devil! and if —"

"Hadn't they better be all together?" interrupted Seth, reminding her of a like epithet used in reference to her little ones.

Without seeming to notice him, she continued, "She can't keep a girl in the house over a week; and Mr. Bellmont wants to hire a boy to work for him, but he can't find one that will live in the house with her; she's so ugly, they can't."

"Well, we've got to make a move soon," answered Seth; "if you go with me, we shall go right off. Had you rather spare the other one?" asked Seth, after a short pause.

"One's as bad as t'other," replied Mag. "Frado is such a wild, frolicky thing, and means to do jest as she's a mind to; she won't go if she don't want to. I don't want to tell her she is to be given away."

"I will," said Seth. "Come here, Frado?"

The child seemed to have some dim foreshadowing of evil, and declined.

"Come here," he continued; "I want to tell you something."

She came reluctantly. He took her hand and said: "We're going to move, by-'m-bye; will you go?"

"No!" screamed she; and giving a sudden jerk which destroyed Seth's equilibrium, left him sprawling on the floor, while she escaped through the open door.

"She's a hard one," said Seth, brushing his patched coat sleeve. "I'd risk her at Bellmont's."

They discussed the expediency of a speedy departure. Seth would first seek employment, and then return for Mag. They would take with them what they could carry, and leave the rest with Pete Greene, and come for them when they were wanted. They were long in arranging affairs satisfactorily, and were not a little startled at the close of their conference to find Frado missing. They thought approaching night would bring her. Twilight passed into darkness, and she did not come.

They thought she had understood their plans, and had, perhaps, permanently withdrawn. They could not rest without making some effort to ascertain her retreat. Seth went in pursuit, and returned without her. They rallied others when they discovered that another little colored girl was missing, a favorite playmate of Frado's. All effort proved unavailing. Mag felt sure her fears were realized, and that she might never see her again. Before her anxieties became realities, both were safely returned, and from them and their attendant they learned that they went to walk, and not minding the direction soon found themselves lost. They had climbed fences and walls, passed through thickets and marshes, and when night approached selected a thick cluster of shrubbery as a covert for the night. They were discovered by the person who now restored them, chatting of their prospects, Frado attempting to banish the childish fears of her companion. As they were some miles from home, they were kindly cared for until morning. Mag was relieved to know her child was not driven to desperation by their intentions to relieve themselves of her, and she was inclined to think severe restraint would be healthful.

The removal was all arranged; the few days necessary for such migrations passed quickly, and one bright summer morning they bade farewell to their Singleton hovel, and with budgets and bundles commenced their weary march. As they neared the village, they heard the merry shouts of children gathered around the schoolroom, awaiting the coming of their teacher.

"Halloo!" screamed one, "Black, white and yeller!" "Black, white and yeller,"[7] echoed a dozen voices.

It did not grate so harshly on poor Mag as once it would. She did not even turn her head to look at them. She had passed into an insensibility no childish taunt could penetrate, else she would have reproached herself as she passed familiar scenes, for extending the separation once so easily annihilated by steadfast integrity. Two miles beyond lived the Bellmonts, in a large, old fashioned, two-story white house, environed by fruitful acres, and embellished by shrubbery and shade trees. Years ago a youthful couple consecrated it as home; and after many little feet had worn paths to favorite fruit trees, and over its green hills, and mingled at last with brother man in the race which belongs neither to the swift or strong, the sire became grey-haired and decrepit, and went to his last repose. His aged consort soon followed him. The old homestead thus passed into the hands of a son, to whose wife Mag had applied the epithet "she-devil," as may be remembered. John, the son, had not in his family arrangements departed from the example of the father. The pastimes of his boyhood were ever freshly revived by witnessing the games of his own sons as they rallied about the same goal his youthful feet had often won; as well as by the amusements of his daughters in their imitations of maternal duties.

At the time we introduce them, however, John is wearing the badge of age. Most of his children were from home; some seeking employment; some were already settled in homes of their own. A maiden sister shared with him the estate on which he resided, and occupied a portion of the house.

Within sight of the house, Seth seated himself with his bundles and the child he had been leading, while Mag walked onward to the house leading Frado. A knock at the door brought Mrs. Bellmont, and Mag asked if she would be willing to let that child stop there while she went to the Reed's house to wash, and when she came back she would call and get her. It seemed a novel request, but she consented. Why the impetuous child entered the house, we cannot tell; the door closed, and Mag hastily departed. Frado waited for the close of day, which was to bring back her mother. Alas! it never came. It was the last time she ever saw or heard of her mother.

CHAPTER III

A New Home for Me

Oh! did we but know of the shadows so nigh,
　The world would indeed be a prison of gloom;
All light would be quenched in youth's eloquent eye,
　And the prayer-lisping infant would ask for the tomb.

For if Hope be a star that may lead us astray,
　And "deceiveth the heart," as the aged ones preach;
Yet 'twas Mercy that gave it, to beacon our way,
　Though its halo illumes where it never can reach.

Eliza Cook [8]

As the day closed and Mag did not appear, surmises were expressed by the family that she never intended to return. Mr. Bellmont was a kind, humane man, who would not grudge hospitality to the poorest wanderer, nor fail to sympathize with any sufferer, however humble. The child's desertion by her mother appealed to his sympathy, and he felt inclined to succor her. To do this in opposition to Mrs. Bellmont's wishes, would be like encountering a whirlwind charged with fire, daggers and spikes. She was not as susceptible of fine emotions as her spouse. Mag's opinion of her was not without foundation. She was self-willed, haughty, undisciplined, arbitrary and severe. In common parlance, she was a *scold,* a thorough one. Mr. B. remained silent during the consultation which follows, engaged in by mother, Mary and John, or Jack, as he was familiarly called.

"Send her to the County House," said Mary, in reply to the query what should be done with her, in a tone which indicated self-importance in the speaker. She was indeed the idol of her mother, and more nearly resembled her in disposition and manners than the others.

Jane, an invalid daughter, the eldest of those at home, was reclining on a sofa apparently uninterested.

"Keep her," said Jack. "She's real handsome and bright, and not very black, either."

"Yes," rejoined Mary; "that's just like you, Jack. She'll be of no use at all these three years, right under foot all the time."

"Poh! Miss Mary; if she should stay, it wouldn't be two days before you would be telling the girls about *our* nig, *our* nig!" retorted Jack.

"I don't want a nigger 'round *me*, do you, mother?" asked Mary.

"I don't mind the nigger in the child. I should like a dozen better than one," replied her mother. "If I could make her do my work in a few years, I would keep her. I have so much trouble with girls I hire, I am almost persuaded if I have one to train up in my way from a child, I shall be able to keep them awhile. I am tired of changing every few months."

"Where could she sleep?" asked Mary. "I don't want her near me."

"In the L chamber," answered the mother.

"How'll she get there?" asked Jack. "She'll be afraid to go through that dark passage, and she can't climb the ladder safely."

"She'll have to go there; it's good enough for a nigger," was the reply.

Jack was sent on horseback to ascertain if Mag was at her home. He returned with the testimony of Pete Greene that they were fairly departed, and that the child was intentionally thrust upon their family.

The imposition was not at all relished by Mrs. B., or the pert, haughty Mary, who had just glided into her teens.

"Show the child to bed, Jack," said his mother. "You seem most pleased with the little nigger, so you may introduce her to her room."

He went to the kitchen, and, taking Frado gently by the hand, told her he would put her in bed now; perhaps her mother would come the next night after her.

It was not yet quite dark, so they ascended the stairs without any light, passing through nicely furnished rooms, which were a source of great amazement to the child. He opened the door which connected with her room by a dark, unfinished passage-way. "Don't bump your head," said Jack, and stepped before to open the door leading into her apartment, – an unfinished chamber over the kitchen, the roof slanting nearly to the floor, so that the bed could stand only in the middle of the room. A small half window furnished light and air. Jack returned to the sitting room with the remark that the child would soon outgrow those quarters.

"When she *does,* she'll outgrow the house," remarked the mother.

"What can she do to help you?" asked Mary. "She came just in the right time, didn't she? Just the very day after Bridget left," continued she.

"I'll see what she can do in the morning," was the answer.

While this conversation was passing below, Frado lay, revolving in her little mind whether she would remain or not until her mother's return. She was of wilful, determined nature, a stranger to fear, and would not hesitate to wander away should she decide to. She remembered the conversation of her mother with Seth, the words "given away" which she heard used in reference to herself, and though she did not know their full import, she thought she should, by remaining, be in some relation to white people she was never favored with before. So she resolved to tarry, with the hope that mother would come and get her some time. The hot sun had penetrated her room, and it was long before a cooling breeze reduced the temperature so that she could sleep.

Frado was called early in the morning by her new mistress. Her first work was to feed the hens. She was shown how it was *always* to be done, and in no other way; any departure from this rule to be punished by a whipping. She was then accompanied by Jack to drive the cows to pasture, so she might learn the way. Upon her return she was allowed to eat her breakfast, consisting of a bowl of skimmed milk, with brown bread crusts, which she was told to eat, standing, by the kitchen table, and must not be over ten minutes about it. Meanwhile the family were taking their morning meal in the dining-room. This over, she was placed on a cricket to wash the common dishes; she was to be in waiting always to bring wood and chips, to run hither and thither from room to room.

A large amount of dish-washing for small hands followed dinner. Then the same after tea and going after the cows finished her first day's work. It was a new discipline to the child. She found some attractions about the place, and she retired to rest at night more willing to remain. The same routine followed day after day, with slight variation; adding a little more work, and spicing the toil with "words that burn," and frequent blows on her head. These were great annoyances to Frado, and had she known where her mother was, she would have gone at once to her. She was often greatly wearied, and silently wept over her sad fate. At first she wept aloud, which Mrs. Bellmont noticed by applying a raw-hide, always at hand in the kitchen. It was a symptom of discontent and complaining which must be "nipped in the bud," she said.

Thus passed a year. No intelligence of Mag. It was now certain Frado was to become a permanent member of the family. Her labors were multiplied; she was quite indispensable, although but seven years old. She had never learned to read, never heard of a school until her residence in the family.

[Mrs. Bellmont was in doubt about the utility of attempting to educate people of color, who were incapable of elevation. This subject occasioned a lengthy discussion in the family. Mr. Bellmont, Jane and Jack arguing for Frado's education; Mary and her mother objecting. At last Mr. Bellmont declared decisively that she *should* go to school.] He was a man who seldom decided controversies at home. The word once spoken admitted of no appeal; so, notwithstanding Mary's objection that she would have to attend the same school she did, the word became law.

It was to be a new scene to Frado, and Jack had many queries and conjectures to answer. He was himself too far advanced to attend the summer school, which Frado regretted, having had too many opportunities of witnessing Miss Mary's temper to feel safe in her company alone.

The opening day of school came. Frado sauntered on far in the rear of Mary, who was ashamed to be seen "walking with a nigger." As soon as she appeared, with scanty clothing and bared feet, the children assembled, noisily published her approach: "See that nigger," shouted one. "Look! look!" cried another. "I won't play with her," said one little girl. "Nor I neither," replied another.

Mary evidently relished these sharp attacks, and saw a fair prospect of lowering Nig where, according to her views, she belonged. Poor Frado, chagrined and grieved, felt that her anticipations of pleasure at such a place were far from being realized. She was just deciding to return home, and never come there again, when the teacher appeared, and observing the downcast looks of the child, took her by the hand, and led her into the school-room. All followed, and, after the bustle of securing seats was over, Miss Marsh inquired if the children knew "any cause for the sorrow of that little girl?" pointing to Frado. It was soon all told. She then reminded them of their duties to the poor and friendless; their cowardice in attacking a young innocent child; referred them to one who looks not on outward appearances, but on the heart. "She looks like a good girl; I think *I* shall love her, so lay aside all prejudice, and vie with each other in shewing kindness and good-will to one who seems different from you," were the closing remarks of the kind lady. Those kind words! The most agreeable sound which ever meets the ear of sorrowing, grieving childhood.

Example rendered her words efficacious. Day by day there was a manifest change of deportment towards "Nig." Her speeches often drew merriment from the children; no one could do more to enliven their favorite pastimes than Frado. Mary could not endure to see her thus noticed, yet knew not how to prevent it. She could not influence her schoolmates as she wished. She had not gained their affections by winning ways and yielding points of controversy. On the contrary, she was self-willed, domineering; every day reported "mad" by some of her companions. She availed herself of the only alternative, abuse and taunts, as they returned from school. This was not satisfactory; she wanted to use physical force "to subdue her," to "keep her down."

There was, on their way home, a field intersected by a stream over which a single plank was placed for a crossing. It occurred to Mary that it would be a punishment to Nig to compel her to cross over; so she dragged her to the edge, and told her authoritatively to go over. Nig hesitated, resisted. Mary placed herself behind the child, and, in the struggle to force her over, lost her footing and plunged into the stream. Some of the larger scholars being in sight, ran, and thus prevented Mary from drowning and Frado from falling. Nig scampered home fast as possible, and Mary went to the nearest house, dripping, to procure a change of garments. She came loitering home, half crying, exclaiming, "Nig pushed me into the stream!" She then related the particulars. Nig was called from the kitchen. Mary stood with anger flashing in her eyes. Mr. Bellmont sat quietly reading his paper. He had witnessed too many of Miss Mary's outbreaks to be startled. Mrs. Bellmont interrogated Nig.

"I didn't do it! I didn't do it!" answered Nig, passionately, and then related the occurrence truthfully.

The discrepancy greatly enraged Mrs. Bellmont. With loud accusations and angry gestures she approached the child. Turning to her husband, she asked,

"Will you sit still, there, and hear that black nigger call Mary a liar?"

"How do we know but she has told the truth? I shall not punish her," he replied, and left the house, as he usually did when a tempest threatened to envelop him. No sooner was he out of sight than Mrs. B. and Mary commenced beating her inhumanly; then propping her mouth open with a piece of wood, shut her up in a dark room, without any supper. For employment, while the tempest raged within, Mr. Bellmont went for the cows, a task belonging to Frado, and thus unintentionally prolonged her pain. At dark Jack came in, and seeing Mary, accosted her with, "So you thought you'd vent your spite on Nig, did you? Why can't you let her alone? It was good enough for you to get a ducking, only you did not stay in half long enough."

Cruel punishment for innocence

"Stop!" said his mother. "You shall never talk so before me. You would have that little nigger trample on Mary, would you? She came home with a lie; it made Mary's story false."

"What was Mary's story?" asked Jack.

It was related.

"Now," said Jack, sallying into a chair, "the school-children happened to see it all, and they tell the same story Nig does. Which is most likely to be true, what a dozen agree they saw, or the contrary?"

"It is very strange you will believe what others say against your sister," retorted his mother, with flashing eye. "I think it is time your father subdued you."

"Father is a sensible man," argued Jack. "He would not wrong a dog. Where *is* Frado?" he continued.

"Mother gave her a good whipping and shut her up," replied Mary.

Just then Mr. Bellmont entered, and asked if Frado was "shut up yet."

The knowledge of her innocence, the perfidy of his sister, worked fearfully on Jack. He bounded from his chair, searched every room till he found the child; her mouth wedged apart, her face swollen, and full of pain.

How Jack pitied her! He relieved her jaws, brought her some supper, took her to her room, comforted her as well as he knew how, sat by her till she fell asleep, and then left for the sitting room. As he passed his mother, he remarked, "If that was the way Frado was to be treated, he hoped she would never wake again!" He then imparted her situation to his father, who seemed untouched, till a glance at Jack exposed a tearful eye. Jack went early to her next morning. She awoke sad, but refreshed. After breakfast Jack took her with him to the field, and kept her through the day. But it could not be so generally. She must return to school, to her household duties. He resolved to do what he could to protect her from Mary and his mother. He bought her a dog, which became a great favorite with both. The invalid, Jane, would gladly befriend her; but she had not the strength to brave the iron will of her mother. Kind words and affectionate glances were the only

Jack consoles Frado by compassionate Frado

expressions of sympathy she could safely indulge in. The men employed on the farm were always glad to hear her prattle; she was a great favorite with them. Mrs. Bellmont allowed them the privilege of talking with her in the kitchen. She did not fear but she should have ample opportunity of subduing her when they were away. Three months of schooling, summer and winter, she enjoyed for three years. Her winter over-dress was a cast-off overcoat, once worn by Jack, and a sun-bonnet. It was a source of great merriment to the scholars, but Nig's retorts were so mirthful, and their satisfaction so evident in attributing the selection to "Old Granny Bellmont," that it was not painful to Nig or pleasurable to Mary. Her jollity was not to be quenched by whipping or scolding. In Mrs. Bellmont's presence she was under restraint; but in the kitchen, and among her schoolmates, the pent up fires burst forth. She was ever at some sly prank when unseen by her teacher, in school hours; not unfrequently some outburst of merriment, of which she was the original, was charged upon some innocent mate, and punishment inflicted which she merited. They enjoyed her antics so fully that any of them would suffer wrongfully to keep open the avenues of mirth. She would venture far beyond propriety, thus shielded and countenanced.

The teacher's desk was supplied with drawers, in which were stored his books and other *et ceteras* of the profession. The children observed Nig very busy there one morning before school, as they flitted in occasionally from their play outside. The master came; called the children to order; opened a drawer to take the book the occasion required; when out poured a volume of smoke. "Fire! fire!" screamed he, at the top of his voice. By this time he had become sufficiently acquainted with the peculiar odor, to know he was imposed upon. The scholars shouted with laughter to see the terror of the dupe, who, feeling abashed at the needless fright, made no very strict investigation, and Nig once more escaped punishment. She had provided herself with cigars, and puffing, puffing away at the crack of the drawer, had filled it with smoke, and then closed it tightly to deceive the teacher, and amuse the scholars. The interim of terms was filled up with a variety of duties new and peculiar.[At home, no matter how powerful the heat when sent to rake hay or guard the grazing herd, she was never permitted to shield her skin from the sun. She was not many shades darker than Mary now; what a calamity it would be ever to hear the contrast spoken of. Mrs. Bellmont was determined the sun should have full power to darken the shade which nature had first bestowed upon her as best befitting.]

Mrs. B purposedly gave her no protection for sun b/c she felt her skin needed darkening → insult that her skin was light like Mary

CHAPTER IV

A Friend for Nig

"Hours of my youth! when nurtured in my breast,
To love a stranger, friendship made me blest; —
Friendship, the dear peculiar bond of youth,
When every artless bosom throbs with truth;
Untaught by worldly wisdom how to feign;
And check each impulse with prudential reign;
When all we feel our honest souls disclose —
In love to friends, in open hate to foes;
No varnished tales the lips of youth repeat,
No dear-bought knowledge purchased by deceit."

Byron [9]

With what differing emotions have the denizens of earth awaited the approach of to-day. Some sufferer has counted the vibrations of the pendulum impatient for its dawn, who, now that it has arrived, is anxious for its close. The votary of pleasure, conscious of yesterday's void, wishes for power to arrest time's haste till a few more hours of mirth shall be enjoyed. The unfortunate are yet gazing in vain for golden-edged clouds they fancied would appear in their horizon. The good man feels that he has accomplished too little for the Master, and sighs that another day must so soon close. Innocent childhood, weary of its stay, longs for another morrow; busy manhood cries, hold! hold! and pursues it to another's dawn. All are dissatisfied. All crave some good not yet possessed, which time is expected to bring with all its morrows.

Was it strange that, to a disconsolate child, three years should seem a long, long time? During school time she had rest from Mrs. Bellmont's tyranny. She was now nine years old; time, her mistress said, such privileges should cease.

[She could now read and spell, and knew the elementary steps in grammar, arithmetic, and writing. Her education completed, as *she* said, Mrs. Bellmont felt that her time and person belonged solely to her. She was under her in every sense of the word. What an opportunity to indulge her vixen nature! No matter what occurred to ruffle her, or from what source provocation came, real or fancied, a few blows on Nig seemed to relieve her of a portion of ill-will.]

These were days when Fido was the entire confidant of Frado. She told him her griefs as though he were human; and he sat so still, and listened so attentively, she really believed he knew her sorrows. All the leisure moments she could gain were used in teaching him some feat of dog-agility, so that Jack pronounced him very knowing, and was truly gratified to know he had furnished her with a gift answering his intentions.

Fido was the constant attendant of Frado, when sent from the house on errands, going and returning with the cows, out in the fields, to the village. If ever she forgot her hardships it was in his company.

Spring was now retiring. James, one of the absent sons, was expected home on a visit. He had never seen the last acquisition to the family. Jack had written faithfully of all the merits of his colored *protegé*, and hinted plainly that mother did not always treat her just right. Many were the preparations to make the visit pleasant, and as the day approached when he was to arrive, great exertions were made to cook the favorite viands, to prepare the choicest table-fare.

The morning of the arrival day was a busy one. Frado knew not who would be of so much importance; her feet were speeding hither and thither so unsparingly. Mrs. Bellmont seemed a trifle fatigued, and her shoes which had, early in the morning, a methodic squeak, altered to an irregular, peevish snap.

"Get some little wood to make the fire burn," said Mrs. Bellmont, in a sharp tone. Frado obeyed, bringing the smallest she could find.

Mrs. Bellmont approached her, and, giving her a box on her ear, reiterated the command.

The first the child brought was the smallest to be found; of course, the second must be a trifle larger. She well knew it was, as she threw it into a box on the hearth. To Mrs. Bellmont it was a greater affront, as well as larger wood, so she "taught her" with the raw-hide, and sent her the third time for "little wood."

Nig, weeping, knew not what to do. She had carried the smallest; none left would suit her mistress; of course further punishment awaited her; so she gathered up whatever came first, and threw it down on the hearth. As she expected, Mrs. Bellmont, enraged, approached her, and kicked her so forcibly as to throw her upon the floor. Before she could rise, another foiled the attempt, and then followed kick after kick in quick succession and power, till she reached the door. Mr. Bellmont and Aunt Abby, hearing the noise, rushed in, just in time to see the last of the performance. Nig jumped up, and rushed from the house, out of sight.

Aunt Abby returned to her apartment, followed by John, who was muttering to himself.

"What were you saying?" asked Aunt Abby.

"I said I hoped the child never would come into the house again."

"What would become of her? You cannot mean *that*," continued his sister.

"I do mean it. The child does as much work as a woman ought to; and just see how she is kicked about!"

"Why do you have it so, John?" asked his sister.

"How am I to help it? Women rule the earth, and all in it."

"I think I should rule my own house, John," –

"And live in hell meantime," added Mr. Bellmont.

John now sauntered out to the barn to await the quieting of the storm.

Aunt Abby had a glimpse of Nig as she passed out of the yard; but to arrest her, or shew her that *she* would shelter her, in Mrs.

Bellmont's presence, would only bring reserved wrath on her defenceless head. Her sister-in-law had great prejudices against her. One cause of the alienation was that she did not give her right in the homestead to John, and leave it forever; another was that she was a professor of religion, (so was Mrs. Bellmont;) but Nab, as she called her, did not live according to her profession; another, that she *would* sometimes give Nig cake and pie, which she was never allowed to have at home. Mary had often noticed and spoken of her inconsistencies.

The dinner hour passed. Frado had not appeared. Mrs. B. made no inquiry or search. Aunt Abby looked long, and found her concealed in an outbuilding. "Come into the house with me," implored Aunt Abby.

"I ain't going in any more," sobbed the child.

"What will you do?" asked Aunt Abby.

"I've got to stay out here and die. I ha'n't got no mother, no home. I wish I was dead."

"Poor thing," muttered Aunt Abby; and slyly providing her with some dinner, left her to her grief.

Jane went to confer with her Aunt about the affair; and learned from her the retreat. She would gladly have concealed her in her own chamber, and ministered to her wants; but she was dependent on Mary and her mother for care, and any displeasure caused by attention to Nig, was seriously felt.

Toward night the coach brought James. A time of general greeting, inquiries for absent members of the family, a visit to Aunt Abby's room, undoing a few delicacies for Jane, brought them to the tea hour.

"Where's Frado?" asked Mr. Bellmont, observing she was not in her usual place, behind her mistress' chair.

"I don't know, and I don't care. If she makes her appearance again, I'll take the skin from her body," replied his wife.

James, a fine looking young man, with a pleasant countenance, placid, and yet decidedly serious, yet not stern, looked up confounded. He was no stranger to his mother's nature; but years of absence had erased the occurrences once so familiar, and he asked, "Is this that pretty little

Nig, Jack writes to me about, that you are so severe upon, mother?"

"I'll not leave much of her beauty to be seen, if she comes in sight; and now, John," said Mrs. B., turning to her husband, "you need not think you are going to learn her to treat me in this way; just see how saucy she was this morning. She shall learn her place."

Mr. Bellmont raised his calm, determined eye full upon her, and said, in a decisive manner: "You shall not strike, or scald, or skin her, as you call it, if she comes back again. Remember!" and he brought his hand down upon the table. "I have searched an hour for her now, and she is not to be found on the premises. Do *you* know where she is? Is she *your* prisoner?"

"No! I have just told you I did not know where she was. Nab has her hid somewhere, I suppose. Oh, dear! I did not think it would come to this; that my own husband would treat me so." Then came fast flowing tears, which no one but Mary seemed to notice. Jane crept into Aunt Abby's room; Mr. Bellmont and James went out of doors, and Mary remained to condole with her parent.

"Do you know where Frado is?" asked Jane of her aunt.

"No," she replied. "I have hunted everywhere. She has left her first hiding-place. I cannot think what has become of her. There comes Jack and Fido; perhaps he knows;" and she walked to a window near, where James and his father were conversing together.

The two brothers exchanged a hearty greeting, and then Mr. Bellmont told Jack to eat his supper; afterward he wished to send him away. He immediately went in. Accustomed to all the phases of indoor storms, from a whine to thunder and lightning, he saw at a glance marks of disturbance. He had been absent through the day, with the hired men.

"What's the fuss?" asked he, rushing into Aunt Abby's.

"Eat your supper," said Jane; "go home, Jack."

Back again through the dining-room, and out to his father.

"What's the fuss?" again inquired he of his father.

"Eat your supper, Jack, and see if you can find Frado. She's not been seen since morning, and then she was kicked out of the house."

"I shan't eat my supper till I find her," said Jack, indignantly. "Come,

James, and see the little creature mother treats so."

They started, calling, searching, coaxing, all their way along. No Frado. They returned to the house to consult. James and Jack declared they would not sleep till she was found.]

Mrs. Bellmont attempted to dissuade them from the search. "It was a shame a little *nigger* should make so much trouble."

Just then Fido came running up, and Jack exclaimed, "Fido knows where she is, I'll bet."

"So I believe," said his father, "but we shall not be wiser unless we can outwit him. He will not do what his mistress forbids him."

"I know how to fix him," said Jack. Taking a plate from the table, which was still waiting, he called, "Fido! Fido! Frado wants some supper. Come!" Jack started, the dog followed, and soon capered on before, far, far into the fields, over walls and through fences, into a piece of swampy land. Jack followed close, and soon appeared to James, who was quite in the rear, coaxing and forcing Frado along with him.

A frail child, driven from shelter by the cruelty of his mother, was an object of interest to James. They persuaded her to go home with them, warmed her by the kitchen fire, gave her a good supper, and took her with them into the sitting room.

"Take that nigger out of my sight," was Mrs. Bellmont's command, before they could be seated.

James led her into Aunt Abby's, where he knew they were welcome. They chatted awhile until Frado seemed cheerful; then James led her to her room, and waited until she retired.

"Are you glad I've come home?" asked James.

"Yes; if you won't let me be whipped tomorrow."

"You won't be whipped. You must try to be a good girl," counselled James.

"If I do, I get whipped;" sobbed the child. "They won't believe what I say. Oh, I wish I had my mother back; then I should not be kicked and whipped so. Who made me so?"

"God;" answered James.

"Did God make you?"

"Yes."

"Who made Aunt Abby?"

"God."

"Who made your mother?"

"God."

"Did the same God that made her make me?"

"Yes."

"Well, then, I don't like him."

"Why not?"

"Because he made her white, and me black. Why didn't he make us *both* white?"

"I don't know; try to go to sleep, and you will feel better in the morning," was all the reply he could make to her knotty queries. It was a long time before she fell asleep; and a number of days before James felt in a mood to visit and entertain old associates and friends.

CHAPTER V

Departures

Life is a strange avenue of various trees and flowers;
Lightsome at commencement, but darkening to its end in a
distant, massy portal.
It beginneth as a little path, edged with the violet and primrose,
A little path of lawny grass and soft to tiny feet.
Soon, spring thistles in the way.

Tupper[10]

James' visit concluded. Frado had become greatly attached to him, and with sorrow she listened and joined in the farewells which preceded his exit. The remembrance of his kindness cheered her through many a weary month, and an occasional word to her in letters to Jack, were like "cold waters to a thirsty soul." Intelligence came that James would soon marry; Frado hoped he would, and remove her from such severe treatment as she was subject to. There had been additional burdens laid on her since his return. She must now *milk* the cows, she had then only to drive. Flocks of sheep had been added to the farm, which daily claimed a portion of her time. In the absence of the men, she must harness the horse for Mary and her mother to ride, go to mill, in short, do the work of a boy, could one be procured to endure the tirades of Mrs. Bellmont. She was first up in the morning, doing what she could towards breakfast. Occasionally, she would utter some funny thing for Jack's benefit, while she was waiting on the table, provoking a sharp look from his mother, or expulsion from the room.

On one such occasion, they found her on the roof of the barn.

Some repairs having been necessary, a staging had been erected, and was not wholly removed. Availing herself of ladders, she was mounted in high glee on the top-most board. Mr. Bellmont called sternly for her to come down; poor Jane nearly fainted from fear. Mrs. B. and Mary did not care if she "broke her neck," while Jack and the men laughed at her fearlessness. Strange, one spark of playfulness could remain amid such constant toil; but her natural temperament was in a high degree mirthful, and the encouragement she received from Jack and the hired men, constantly nurtured the inclination. When she had none of the family around to be merry with, she would amuse herself with the animals. Among the sheep was a willful leader, who always persisted in being first served, and many times in his fury he had thrown down Nig, till, provoked, she resolved to punish him. The pasture in which the sheep grazed was bounded on three sides by a wide stream, which flowed on one side at the base of precipitous banks. The first spare moments at her command, she ran to the pasture with a dish in her hand, and mounting the highest point of land nearest the stream, called the flock to their mock repast. Mr. Bellmont, with his laborers, were in sight, though unseen by Frado. They paused to see what she was about to do. Should she by any mishap lose her footing, she must roll into the stream, and, without aid, must drown. They thought of shouting; but they feared an unexpected salute might startle her, and thus ensure what they were anxious to prevent. They watched in breathless silence. The willful sheep came furiously leaping and bounding far in advance of the flock. Just as he leaped for the dish, she suddenly jumped one side, when down he rolled into the river, and swimming across, remained alone till night. The men lay down, convulsed with laughter at the trick, and guessed at once its object. Mr. Bellmont talked seriously to the child for exposing herself to such danger; but she hopped about on her toes, and with laughable grimaces replied, she knew she was quick enough to "give him a slide."

But to return. James married a Baltimorean lady of wealthy parentage, an indispensable requisite, his mother had always taught him. He did not marry her wealth, though; he loved *her,* sincerely. She was not unlike his sister Jane, who had a social, gentle, loving nature, rather *too* yielding, her brother thought. His Susan had a firmness which Jane needed to complete her character, but which her ill health may in a measure have failed to produce. Although an invalid, she was not excluded from society. Was it strange *she* should seem a desirable companion, a treasure as a wife?

Two young men seemed desirous of possessing her. One was a neighbor, Henry Reed, a tall, spare young man, with sandy hair, and blue, sinister eyes. He seemed to appreciate her wants, and watch with interest her improvement or decay. His kindness she received, and by it was almost won. Her mother wished her to encourage his attentions. She had counted the acres which were to be transmitted to an only son; she knew there was silver in the purse; she would not have Jane too sentimental.

The eagerness with which he amassed wealth, was repulsive to Jane; he did not spare his person or beasts in its pursuit. She felt that to such a man she should be considered an incumbrance; she doubted if he would desire her, if he did not know she would bring a handsome patrimony. Her mother, full in favor with the parents of Henry, commanded her to accept him. She engaged herself, yielding to her mother's wishes, because she had not strength to oppose them; and sometimes, when witness of her mother's and Mary's tyranny, she felt any change would be preferable, even such a one as this. She knew her husband should be the man of her own selecting, one she was conscious of preferring before all others. She could not say this of Henry.

In this dilemma, a visitor came to Aunt Abby's; one of her boy-favorites, George Means, from an adjoining State. Sensible, plain looking, agreeable, talented, he could not long be a stranger to any one who wished to know him. Jane was accustomed to sit much with Aunt Abby always; her presence now seemed necessary to assist in entertaining this youthful friend. Jane was more pleased with him each day, and silently wished Henry possessed more refinement, and the polished manners of George. She felt dissatisfied with her relation to him. His calls while George was there, brought their opposing qualities vividly before her, and she found it disagreeable to force herself into those attentions belonging to him. She received him apparently only as a neighbor.

George returned home, and Jane endeavored to stifle the risings of dissatisfaction, and had nearly succeeded, when a letter came which needed but one glance to assure her of its birth-place; and she retired for its perusal. Well was it for her that her mother's suspicion was not aroused, or her curiosity startled to inquire who it came from. After reading it, she glided into Aunt Abby's, and placed it in her hands, who was no stranger to Jane's trials.

George could not rest after his return, he wrote, until he had communicated to Jane the emotions her presence awakened, and his desire to love and possess her as his own. He begged to know if his affections were reciprocated, or could be; if she would permit him to write to her; if she was free from all obligation to another.

"What would mother say?" queried Jane, as she received the letter from her aunt.

"Not much to comfort you."

"Now, aunt, George is just such a man as I could really love, I think, from all I have seen of him; you know I never could say that of Henry" –

"Then don't marry him," interrupted Aunt Abby.

"Mother will make me."

"Your father won't."

"Well, aunt, what can I do? Would you answer the letter, or not?"

"Yes, answer it. Tell him your situation."

"I shall not tell him all my feelings."

Jane answered that she had enjoyed his company much; she had seen nothing offensive in his manner or appearance; that she was under no obligations which forbade her receiving letters from him as a friend and acquaintance. George was puzzled by the reply. He wrote to Aunt Abby, and from her learned all. He could not see Jane thus sacrificed, without making an effort to rescue her. Another visit followed. George heard Jane say she preferred *him*. He then conferred with Henry at his home. It was not a pleasant subject to talk upon. To be thus supplanted, was not to be thought of. He would sacrifice everything but his inheritance to secure his betrothed.

"And so you are the cause of her late coldness towards me. Leave! I will talk no more about it; the business is settled between us; there it will remain," said Henry.

"Have you no wish to know the real state of Jane's affections towards you?" asked George.

"No! Go, I say! go!" and Henry opened the door for him to pass out.

He retired to Aunt Abby's. Henry soon followed, and presented his cause to Mrs. Bellmont.

Provoked, surprised, indignant, she summoned Jane to her presence, and after a lengthy tirade upon Nab, and her satanic influence, told her she could not break the bonds which held her to Henry; she should not. George Means was rightly named; he was, truly, mean enough; she knew his family of old; his father had four wives, and five times as many children.

"Go to your room, Miss Jane," she continued. "Don't let me know of your being in Nab's for one while."

The storm was now visible to all beholders. Mr. Bellmont sought Jane. She told him her objections to Henry; showed him George's letter; told her answer, the occasion of his visit. He bade her not make herself sick; he would see that she was not compelled to violate her free choice in so important a transaction. He then sought the two young men; told them he could not as a father see his child compelled to an uncongenial union; a free, voluntary choice was of such importance to one of her health. She must be left free to her own choice.

Jane sent Henry a letter of dismission; he her one of a legal bearing, in which he balanced his disappointment by a few hundreds.

To brave her mother's fury, nearly overcame her, but the consolations of a kind father and aunt cheered her on. After a suitable interval she was married to George, and removed to his home in Vermont. Thus

another light disappeared from Nig's horizon. Another was soon to
follow. Jack was anxious to try his skill in providing for his own
support; so a situation as clerk in a store was procured in a Western
city, and six months after Jane's departure, was Nig abandoned to the
tender mercies of Mary and her mother. As if to remove the last vestige
of earthly joy, Mrs. Bellmont sold the companion and pet of Frado,
the dog Fido.

CHAPTER VI

Varieties

"Hard are life's early steps; and but that youth is
buoyant, confident, and strong in hope, men would
behold its threshold and despair." [11]

The sorrow of Frado was very great for her pet, and Mr. Bellmont
by great exertion obtained it again, much to the relief of the child.
To be thus deprived of all her sources of pleasure was a sure way to
exalt their worth, and Fido became, in her estimation, a more valuable
presence than the human beings who surrounded her.[12]

James had now been married a number of years, and frequent
requests for a visit from the family were at last accepted, and Mrs.
Bellmont made great preparations for a fall sojourn in Baltimore. Mary
was installed housekeeper – in name merely, for Nig was the only
moving power in the house. Although suffering from their joint severity,
she felt safer than to be thrown wholly upon an ardent, passionate,
unrestrained young lady, whom she always hated and felt it hard to be
obliged to obey. The trial she must meet. Were Jack or Jane at home
she would have some refuge; one only remained; good Aunt Abby was
still in the house.

She saw the fast receding coach which conveyed her master and
mistress with regret, and begged for one favor only, that James would
send for her when they returned, a hope she had confidently cherished
all these five years.

She was now able to do all the washing, ironing, baking, and the
common *et cetera* of house-hold duties, though but fourteen. Mary left

all for her to do, though she affected great responsibility. She would show herself in the kitchen long enough to relieve herself of some command, better withheld; or insist upon some compliance to her wishes in some department which she was very imperfectly acquainted with, very much less than the person she was addressing; and so impetuous till her orders were obeyed, that to escape the turmoil, Nig would often go contrary to her own knowledge to gain a respite.

Nig was taken sick! What could be done? The *work*, certainly, but not by Miss Mary. So Nig would work while she could remain erect, then sink down upon the floor, or a chair, till she could rally for a fresh effort. Mary would look in upon her, chide her for her laziness, threaten to tell mother when she came home, and so forth.

"Nig!" screamed Mary, one of her sickest days, "come here, and sweep these threads from the carpet." She attempted to drag her weary limbs along, using the broom as support. Impatient of delay, she called again, but with a different request. "Bring me some wood, you lazy jade, quick." Nig rested the broom against the wall, and started on the fresh behest.

Too long gone. Flushed with anger, she rose and greeted her with, "What are you gone so long, for? Bring it in quick, I say."

"I am coming as quick as I can," she replied, entering the door.

"Saucy, impudent nigger, you! is this the way you answer me?" and taking a large carving knife from the table, she hurled it, in her rage, at the defenceless girl.

Dodging quickly, it fastened in the ceiling a few inches from where she stood. There rushed on Mary's mental vision a picture of bloodshed,[13] in which she was the perpetrator, and the sad consequences of what was so nearly an actual occurrence.

"Tell anybody of this, if you dare. If you tell Aunt Abby, I'll certainly kill you," said she, terrified. She returned to her room, brushed her threads herself; was for a day or two more guarded, and so escaped deserved and merited penalty.

Oh, how long the weeks seemed which held Nig in subjection to Mary; but they passed like all earth's sorrows and joys. Mr. and Mrs.

B. returned delighted with their visit, and laden with rich presents for Mary. No word of hope for Nig. James was quite unwell, and would come home the next spring for a visit.

This, thought Nig, will be my time of release. I shall go back with him.

From early dawn until after all were retired, was she toiling, overworked, disheartened, longing for relief.

Exposure from heat to cold, or the reverse, often destroyed her health for short intervals. She wore no shoes until after frost, and snow even, appeared; and bared her feet again before the last vestige of winter disappeared. These sudden changes she was so illy guarded against, nearly conquered her physical system. Any word of complaint was severely repulsed or cruelly punished.

She was told she had much more than she deserved. So that manual labor was not in reality her only burden; but such an incessant torrent of scolding and boxing and threatening, was enough to deter one of maturer years from remaining within sound of the strife.

It is impossible to give an impression of the manifest enjoyment of Mrs. B. in these kitchen scenes. [It was her favorite exercise to enter the apartment noisily, vociferate orders, give a few sudden blows to quicken Nig's pace, then return to the sitting room with *such* a satisfied expression, congratulating herself upon her thorough house-keeping qualities.] Mrs. B's torments

She usually rose in the morning at the ringing of the bell for breakfast; if she were heard stirring before that time, Nig knew well there was an extra amount of scolding to be borne.

No one now stood between herself and Frado, but Aunt Abby. And if *she* dared to interfere in the least, she was ordered back to her "own quarters." Nig would creep slyly into her room, learn what she could of her regarding the absent, and thus gain some light in the thick gloom of care and toil and sorrow in which she was immersed.

The first of spring a letter came from James, announcing declining health. He must try northern air as a restorative; so Frado joyfully prepared for this agreeable increase of the family, this addition to her cares.

He arrived feeble, lame, from his disease, so changed Frado wept at his appearance, fearing he would be removed from her forever. He kindly greeted her, took her to the parlor to see his wife and child, and said many things to kindle smiles on her sad face.

Frado felt so happy in his presence, so safe from maltreatment! He was to her a shelter. He observed, silently, the ways of the house a few days; Nig still took her meals in the same manner as formerly, having the same allowance of food. He, one day, bade her not remove the food, but sit down to the table and eat.

"She *will*, mother," said he, calmly, but imperatively; "I'm determined; she works hard; I've watched her. Now, while I stay, she is going to sit down *here*, and eat such food as we eat."

A few sparks from the mother's black eyes were the only reply; she feared to oppose where she knew she could not prevail. So Nig's standing attitude, and selected diet vanished.

Her clothing was yet poor and scanty; she was not blessed with a Sunday attire; for she was never permitted to attend church with her mistress. "Religion was not meant for niggers," *she* said; when the husband and brothers were absent, she would drive Mrs. B. and Mary there, then return, and go for them at the close of the service, but never remain. Aunt Abby would take her to evening meetings, held in the neighborhood, which Mrs. B. never attended; and impart to her lessons of truth and grace as they walked to the place of prayer.

Many of less piety would scorn to present so doleful a figure; Mrs. B. had shaved her glossy ringlets; and, in her coarse cloth gown and ancient bonnet, she was anything but an enticing object. But Aunt Abby looked within. She saw a soul to save, an immortality of happiness to secure.

These evenings were eagerly anticipated by Nig; it was such a pleasant release from labor.

Such perfect contrast in the melody and prayers of these good people to the harsh tones which fell on her ears during the day.

Soon she had all their sacred songs at command, and enlivened her toil by accompanying it with this melody.

James encouraged his aunt in her efforts. He had found the *Saviour*, he wished to have Frado's desolate heart gladdened, quieted, sustained, by *His* presence. He felt sure there were elements in her heart which, transformed and purified by the gospel, would make her worthy the esteem and friendship of the world. A kind, affectionate heart, native wit, and common sense, and the pertness she sometimes exhibited, he felt if restrained properly, might become useful in originating a self-reliance which would be of service to her in after years.

Yet it was not possible to compass all this, while she remained where she was. He wished to be cautious about pressing too closely her claims on his mother, as it would increase the burdened one he so anxiously wished to relieve. He cheered her on with the hope of returning with his family, when he recovered sufficiently.

Nig seemed awakened to new hopes and aspirations, and realized a longing for the future, hitherto unknown.

To complete Nig's enjoyment, Jack arrived unexpectedly. His greeting was as hearty to herself as to any of the family.

"Where are your curls, Fra?" asked Jack, after the usual salutation. "Your mother cut them off?"

"Thought you were getting handsome, did she? Same old story, is it; knocks and bumps? Better times coming; never fear, Nig."

How different this appellative sounded from him; he said it in such a tone, with such a rogueish look!

She laughed, and replied that he had better take her West for a housekeeper.

Jack was pleased with James's innovations of table discipline, and would often tarry in the dining-room, to see Nig in her new place at the family table. As he was thus sitting one day, after the family had finished dinner, Frado seated herself in her mistress' chair, and was just reaching for a clean dessert plate which was on the table, when her mistress entered.

"Put that plate down; you shall not have a clean one; eat from mine," continued she. Nig hesitated. To eat after James, his wife or Jack, would have been pleasant; but to be commanded to do what was disagreeable by her mistress, *because* it was disagreeable, was trying. Quickly looking about, she took the plate, called Fido to wash it, which he did to the best of his ability; then, wiping her knife and fork on the cloth, she proceeded to eat her dinner.

Nig never looked toward her mistress during the process. She had Jack near; she did not fear her now.

Insulted, full of rage, Mrs. Bellmont rushed to her husband, and commanded him to notice this insult; to whip that child; if he would not do it, James ought.

James came to hear the kitchen version of the affair. Jack was boiling over with laughter. He related all the circumstances to James, and pulling a bright, silver half-dollar from his pocket, he threw it at Nig, saying, "There, take that; 'twas worth paying for."

James sought his mother; told her he "would not excuse or palliate Nig's impudence; but she should not be whipped or be punished at all. You have not treated her, mother, so as to gain her love; she is only exhibiting your remissness in this matter."

She only smothered her resentment until a convenient opportunity offered. The first time she was left alone with Nig, she gave her a thorough beating, to bring up arrearages; and threatened, if she ever exposed her to James, she would "cut her tongue out."

James found her, upon his return, sobbing; but fearful of revenge, she dared not answer his queries. He guessed their cause, and longed for returning health to take her under his protection.

CHAPTER VII

Spiritual Condition of Nig

"What are our joys but dreams? and what our hopes
But goodly shadows in the summer cloud?"

H. K. W.[14]

James did not improve as was hoped. Month after month passed away, and brought no prospect of returning health. He could not walk far from the house for want of strength; but he loved to sit with Aunt Abby in her quiet room, talking of unseen glories, and heart-experiences, while planning for the spiritual benefit of those around them. In these confidential interviews, Frado was never omitted. They would discuss the prevalent opinion of the public, that people of color are really inferior; incapable of cultivation and refinement. They would glance at the qualities of Nig, which promised so much if rightly directed. "I wish you would take her, James, when you are well, home with *you*," said Aunt Abby, in one of these seasons.

"Just what I am longing to do, Aunt Abby. Susan is just of my mind, and we intend to take her; I have been wishing to do so for years."

"She seems much affected by what she hears at the evening meetings, and asks me many questions on serious things; seems to love to read the Bible; I feel hopes of her."

"I hope she *is* thoughtful; no one has a kinder heart, one capable of loving more devotedly. But to think how prejudiced the world are towards her people; that she must be reared in such ignorance as to drown all the finer feelings. When I think of what she might be, of what she will be, I feel like grasping time till opinions change, and thousands like her rise into a noble freedom. I have seen Frado's grief, because she is black, amount to agony. It makes me sick to recall these scenes. Mother pretends to think she don't know enough to sorrow for anything; but if she could see her as I have, when she supposed herself entirely alone, except her little dog Fido, lamenting her loneliness and complexion, I think, if she is not past feeling, she would retract. In the summer I was walking near the barn, and as I stood I heard sobs. 'Oh! oh!' I heard, 'why was I made? why can't I die? Oh, what have I to live for? No one cares for me only to get my work. And I feel sick; who cares for that? Work as long as I can stand, and then fall down and lay there till I can get up. No mother, father, brother or sister to care for me, and then it is, You lazy nigger, lazy nigger – all because I am black! Oh, if I could die!'

"I stepped into the barn, where I could see her. She was crouched down by the hay with her faithful friend Fido, and as she ceased speaking, buried her face in her hands, and cried bitterly; then, patting Fido, she kissed him, saying, 'You love me, Fido, don't you? but we must go work in the field.' She started on her mission; I called her to me, and told her she need not go, the hay was doing well.

"She has such confidence in me that she will do just as I tell her; so we found a seat under a shady tree, and there I took the opportunity to combat the notions she seemed to entertain respecting the loneliness of her condition and want of sympathizing friends. I assured her that mother's views were by no means general; that in our part of the country there were thousands upon thousands who favored the elevation of her race, disapproving of oppression in all its forms; that she was not unpitied, friendless, and utterly despised; that she might hope for better things in the future. Having spoken these words of comfort, I rose with the resolution that if I recovered my health I would take her home with me, whether mother was willing or not."

"I don't know what your mother would do without her; still, I wish she was away."

Susan now came for her long absent husband, and they returned home to their room.

The month of November was one of great anxiety on James's account. He was rapidly wasting away.

A celebrated physician was called, and performed a surgical operation, as a last means. Should this fail, there was no hope. Of course he was confined wholly to his room, mostly to his bed. With all his bodily suffering, all his anxiety for his family, whom he might not live to protect, he did not forget Frado. He shielded her from many beatings, and every day imparted religious instructions. No one, but his wife, could move him so easily as Frado; so that in addition to her daily toil she was often deprived of her rest at night.

Yet she insisted on being called; she wished to show her love for one who had been such a friend to her. Her anxiety and grief increased as the probabilities of his recovery became doubtful.

Mrs. Bellmont found her weeping on his account, shut her up, and whipped her with the raw-hide, adding an injunction never to be seen snivelling again because she had a little work to do. She was very careful never to shed tears on his account, in her presence, afterwards.

CHAPTER VIII

Visitor and Departure

– "Other cares engross me, and my tired soul with emulative haste, Looks to its God." [15]

The brother associated with James in business, in Baltimore, was sent for to confer with one who might never be able to see him there.

James began to speak of life as closing; of heaven, as of a place in immediate prospect; of aspirations, which waited for fruition in glory. His brother, Lewis by name, was an especial favorite of sister Mary; more like her, in disposition and preferences than James or Jack.

He arrived as soon as possible after the request, and saw with regret the sure indications of fatality in his sick brother, and listened to his admonitions – admonitions to a Christian life – with tears, and uttered some promises of attention to the subject so dear to the heart of James.

How gladly he would have extended healing aid. But, alas! it was not in his power; so, after listening to his wishes and arrangements for his family and business, he decided to return home.

Anxious for company home, he persuaded his father and mother to permit Mary to attend him. She was not at all needed in the sick room; she did not choose to be useful in the kitchen, and then she was fully determined to go.

So all the trunks were assembled and crammed with the best selections from the wardrobe of herself and mother, where the last-mentioned articles could be appropriated.

"Nig was never so helpful before," Mary remarked, and wondered what had induced such a change in place of former sullenness.

Nig was looking further than the present, and congratulating herself upon some days of peace, for Mary never lost opportunity of informing her mother of Nig's delinquencies, were she otherwise ignorant.

Was it strange if she were officious, with such relief in prospect?

The parting from the sick brother was tearful and sad. James prayed in their presence for their renewal in holiness; and urged their immediate attention to eternal realities, and gained a promise that Susan and Charlie should share their kindest regards.

No sooner were they on their way, than Nig slyly crept round to Aunt Abby's room, and tip-toeing and twisting herself into all shapes, she exclaimed, —

"She's gone, Aunt Abby, she's gone, fairly gone;" and jumped up and down, till Aunt Abby feared she would attract the notice of her mistress by such demonstrations.

"Well, she's gone, gone, Aunt Abby. I hope she'll never come back again."

"No! no! Frado, that's wrong! you would be wishing her dead; that won't do."

"Well, I'll bet she'll never come back again; somehow, I feel as though she wouldn't."

"She is James's sister," remonstrated Aunt Abby.

"So is our cross sheep just as much, that I ducked in the river; I'd like to try my hand at curing *her* too."

"But you forget what our good minister told us last week, about doing good to those that hate us."

"Didn't I do good, Aunt Abby, when I washed and ironed and packed her old duds to get rid of her, and helped her pack her trunks, and run here and there for her?"

"Well, well, Frado; you must go finish your work, or your mistress will be after you, and remind you severely of Miss Mary, and some others beside."

Nig went as she was told, and her clear voice was heard as she went, singing in joyous notes the relief she felt at the removal of one of her tormentors.

Day by day the quiet of the sick man's room was increased. He was helpless and nervous; and often wished change of position, thereby hoping to gain momentary relief. The calls upon Frado were consequently more frequent, her nights less tranquil. Her health was impaired by lifting the sick man, and by drudgery in the kitchen. Her ill health she endeavored to conceal from James, fearing he might have less repose if there should be a change of attendants; and Mrs. Bellmont, she well knew, would have no sympathy for her. She was at last so much reduced as to be unable to stand erect for any great length of time. She would *sit* at the table to wash her dishes; if she heard the well-known step of her mistress, she would rise till she returned to her room, and then sink down for further rest. Of course she was longer than usual in completing the services assigned her. This was a subject of complaint to Mrs. Bellmont; and Frado endeavored to throw off all appearance of sickness in her presence.

But it was increasing upon her, and she could no longer hide her indisposition. Her mistress entered one day, and finding her seated, commanded her to go to work. "I am sick," replied Frado, rising and walking slowly to her unfinished task, "and cannot stand long, I feel so bad."

Angry that she should venture a reply to her command, she suddenly inflicted a blow which lay the tottering girl prostrate on the floor. Excited by so much indulgence of a dangerous passion, she seemed left to unrestrained malice; and snatching a towel, stuffed the mouth of the sufferer, and beat her cruelly.

Frado hoped she would end her misery by whipping her to death. She bore it with the hope of a martyr, that her misery would soon close. Though her mouth was muffled, and the sounds much stifled, there was a sensible commotion, which James' quick ear detected.

"Call Frado to come here," he said faintly, "I have not seen her to-day."

Susan retired with the request to the kitchen, where it was evident some brutal scene had just been enacted.

Mrs. Bellmont replied that she had "some work to do just now; when that was done, she might come."

Susan's appearance confirmed her husband's fears, and he requested his father, who sat by the bedside, to go for her. This was a messenger, as James well knew, who could not be denied; and the girl entered the room, sobbing and faint with anguish.

James called her to him, and inquired the cause of her sorrow. She was afraid to expose the cruel author of her misery, lest she should provoke new attacks. But after much entreaty, she told him all, much which had escaped his watchful ear. Poor James shut his eyes in silence, as if pained to forgetfulness by the recital. Then turning to Susan, he asked her to take Charlie, and walk out; "she needed the fresh air," he said. "And say to mother I wish Frado to sit by me till you return. I think you are fading, from staying so long in this sick room." Mr. B. also left, and Frado was thus left alone with her friend. Aunt Abby came in to make her daily visit, and seeing the sick countenance of the attendant, took her home with her to administer some cordial. She soon returned, however, and James kept her with him the rest of the day; and a comfortable night's repose following, she was enabled to continue, as usual, her labors. James insisted on her attending religious meetings in the vicinity with Aunt Abby.

Frado, under the instructions of Aunt Abby and the minister, became a believer in a future existence – one of happiness or misery. Her doubt was, *is* there a heaven for the black? She knew there was one for James, and Aunt Abby, and all good white people; but was there any for blacks? She had listened attentively to all the minister said, and all Aunt Abby had told her; but then it was all for white people.[16]

As James approached that blessed world, she felt a strong desire to follow, and be with one who was such a dear, kind friend to her.

While she was exercised with these desires and aspirations, she attended an evening meeting with Aunt Abby, and the good man urged all, young or old, to accept the offers of mercy, to receive a compassionate Jesus as their Saviour. "Come to Christ," he urged, "all, young or old, white or black, bond or free, come all to Christ for pardon; repent, believe."

This was the message she longed to hear; it seemed to be spoken for her. But he had told them to repent; "what was that?" she asked. She knew she was unfit for any heaven, made for whites or blacks. She would gladly repent, or do anything which would admit her to share the abode of James.

Her anxiety increased; her countenance bore marks of solicitude unseen before; and though she said nothing of her inward contest, they all observed a change.

James and Aunt Abby hoped it was the springing of good seed sown by the Spirit of God. Her tearful attention at the last meeting encouraged his aunt to hope that her mind was awakened, her conscience aroused. Aunt Abby noticed that she was particularly engaged in reading the Bible; and this strengthened her conviction that a heavenly Messenger was striving with her. The neighbors dropped in to inquire after the sick, and also if Frado was "*serious?*" They noticed she seemed very thoughtful and tearful at the meetings. Mrs. Reed was very inquisitive; but Mrs. Bellmont saw no appearance of change for the better. She did not feel responsible for her spiritual culture, and hardly believed she had a soul.

Nig was in truth suffering much; her feelings were very intense on any subject, when once aroused. She read her Bible carefully, and as often as an opportunity presented, which was when entirely secluded in her own apartment, or by Aunt Abby's side, who kindly directed her to Christ, and instructed her in the way of salvation.

Mrs. Bellmont found her one day quietly reading her Bible. Amazed and half crediting the reports of officious neighbors, she felt it was time to interfere. Here she was, reading and shedding tears over the Bible. She ordered her to put up the book, and go to work, and not be snivelling about the house, or stop to read again.

But there was one little spot seldom penetrated by her mistress' watchful eye: this was her room, uninviting and comfortless; but to herself a safe retreat. Here she would listen to the pleadings of a Saviour, and try to penetrate the veil of doubt and sin which clouded her soul, and long to cast off the fetters of sin, and rise to the communion of saints.

Mrs. Bellmont, as we before said, did not trouble herself about the future destiny of her servant. If she did what she desired for *her* benefit, it was all the responsibility she acknowledged. But she seemed to have great aversion to the notice Nig would attract should she become pious. How could she meet this case? She resolved to make her complaint to John. Strange, when she was always foiled in this direction, she should resort to him. It was time something was done; she had begun to read the Bible openly.

The night of this discovery, as they were retiring, Mrs. Bellmont introduced the conversation, by saying:

"I want your attention to what I am going to say. I have let Nig go out to evening meetings a few times, and, if you will believe it, I found her reading the Bible to-day, just as though she expected to turn pious nigger, and preach to white folks. So now you see what good comes of sending her to school. If she should get converted she would have to go to meeting: at least, as long as James lives. I wish he had not such queer notions about her. It seems to trouble him to know he must die and leave her. He says if he should get well he would take her home with him, or educate her here. Oh, how awful! What can the child mean? So careful, too, of her! He says we shall ruin her health making her work so hard, and sleep in such a place. O, John! do you think he is in his right mind?"

"Yes, yes; she is slender."

"Yes, *yes!*" she repeated sarcastically, "you know these niggers are just like black snakes; you *can't* kill them. If she wasn't tough she would have been killed long ago. There was never one of my girls could do half the work."

"Did they ever try?" interposed her husband. "I think she can do more than all of them together."

"What a man!" said she, peevishly. "But I want to know what is going to be done with her about getting pious?"

"Let her do just as she has a mind to. If it is a comfort to her, let her enjoy the privilege of being good. I see no objection."

"I should think *you* were crazy, sure. Don't you know that every night she will want to go toting off to meeting? and Sundays, too? and you know we have a great deal of company Sundays, and she can't be spared."

"I thought you Christians held to going to church," remarked Mr. B.

"Yes, but who ever thought of having a nigger go, except to drive others there? Why, according to you and James, we should very soon have her in the parlor, as smart as our own girls. It's of no use talking to you or James. If you should go on as you would like, it would not be six months before she would be leaving me; and that won't do. Just think how much profit she was to us last summer. We had no work hired out; she did the work of two girls –"

"And got the whippings for two with it!" remarked Mr. Bellmont.

"I'll beat the money out of her, if I can't get her worth any other way,"[17] retorted Mrs. B. sharply. While this scene was passing, Frado was trying to utter the prayer of the publican, "God be merciful to me a sinner."[18]

Bellmont have no true ownership over Frado but have bondaged her mentally to believe SD

CHAPTER IX

Death

We have now
But a small portion of what men call time,
To hold communion.[19]

Spring opened, and James, instead of rallying, as was hoped, grew worse daily. Aunt Abby and Frado were the constant allies of Susan. Mrs. Bellmont dared not lift him. She was not "strong enough," she said.

It was very offensive to Mrs. B. to have Nab about James so much. She had thrown out many a hint to detain her from so often visiting the sick-room; but Aunt Abby was too well accustomed to her ways to mind them. After various unsuccessful efforts, she resorted to the following expedient. As she heard her cross the entry below, to ascend the stairs, she slipped out and held the latch of the door which led into the upper entry.

"James does not want to see you, or any one else," she said.

Aunt Abby hesitated, and returned slowly to her own room; wondering if it were really James' wish not to see her. She did not venture again that day, but still felt disturbed and anxious about him. She inquired of Frado, and learned that he was no worse. She asked her if James did not wish her to come and see him; what could it mean?

Quite late next morning, Susan came to see what had become of her aunt.

"Your mother said James did not wish to see me, and I was afraid

I tired him."

"Why, aunt, that is a mistake, I *know*. What could mother mean?" asked Susan.

The next time she went to the sitting-room she asked her mother, –

"Why does not Aunt Abby visit James as she has done? Where is she?"

"At home. I hope that she will stay there," was the answer.

"I should think she would come in and see James," continued Susan.

"I told her he did not want to see her, and to stay out. You need make no stir about it; remember:" she added, with one of her fiery glances.

Susan kept silence. It was a day or two before James spoke of her absence. The family were at dinner, and Frado was watching beside him. He inquired the cause of her absence, and *she* told him all. After the family returned he sent his wife for her. When she entered, he took her hand, and said, "Come to me often, Aunt. Come any time, – I am always glad to see you. I have but a little longer to be with you, – come often, Aunt. Now please help lift me up, and see if I can rest a little."

Frado was called in, and Susan and Mrs. B. all attempted; Mrs. B. was too weak; she did not feel able to lift so much. So the three succeeded in relieving the sufferer.

Frado returned to her work. Mrs. B. followed. Seizing Frado, she said she would "cure her of tale-bearing," and, placing the wedge of wood between her teeth, she beat her cruelly with the raw-hide. Aunt Abby heard the blows, and came to see if she could hinder them.

Surprised at her sudden appearance, Mrs. B. suddenly stopped, but forbade her removing the wood till she gave her permission, and commanded Nab to go home.[20]

She was thus tortured when Mr. Bellmont came in, and, making inquiries which she did not, because she could not, answer, approached her; and seeing her situation, quickly removed the instrument of torture, and sought his wife. Their conversation we will omit; suffice it to say, a storm raged which required many days to exhaust its strength.

Frado was becoming seriously ill. She had no relish for food, and was constantly overworked, and then she had such solicitude about the future. She wished to pray for pardon. She did try to pray. Her mistress had told her it would "do no good for her to attempt prayer; prayer was for whites, not for blacks. If she minded her mistress, and did what she commanded, it was all that was required of her."

This did not satisfy her, or appease her longings. She knew her instructions did not harmonize with those of the man of God or Aunt Abby's. She resolved to persevere. She said nothing on the subject, unless asked. It was evident to all her mind was deeply exercised. James longed to speak with her alone on the subject. An opportunity presented soon, while the family were at tea. It was usual to summon Aunt Abby to keep company with her, as his death was expected hourly.

As she took her accustomed seat, he asked, "Are you afraid to stay with me alone, Frado?"

"No," she replied, and stepped to the window to conceal her emotion.

"Come here, and sit by me; I wish to talk with you."

She approached him, and, taking her hand, he remarked:

"How poor you are, Frado! I want to tell you that I fear I shall never be able to talk with you again. It is the last time, perhaps, I shall ever talk with you. You are old enough to remember my dying words and profit by them. I have been sick a long time; I shall die pretty soon. My Heavenly Father is calling me home. Had it been his will to let me live I should take you to live with me; but, as it is, I shall go and leave you. But, Frado, if you will be a good girl, and love and serve God, it will be but a short time before we are in a *heavenly* home together. There will never be any sickness or sorrow there."

Frado, overcome with grief, sobbed, and buried her face in his pillow. She expected he would die; but to hear him speak of his departure himself was unexpected.

"Bid me good bye, Frado."

She kissed him, and sank on her knees by his bedside; his hand rested on her head; his eyes were closed; his lips moved in prayer for this disconsolate child.

His wife entered, and interpreting the scene, gave him some restoratives, and withdrew for a short time.

It was a great effort for Frado to cease sobbing; but she dared not be seen below in tears; so she choked her grief, and descended to her usual toil. Susan perceived a change in her husband. She felt that death was near.

He tenderly looked on her, and said, "Susan, my wife, our farewells are all spoken. I feel prepared to go. I shall meet you in heaven. Death is indeed creeping fast upon me. Let me see them all once more. Teach Charlie the way to heaven; lead him up as you come."

The family all assembled. He could not talk as he wished to them. He seemed to sink into unconsciousness. They watched him for hours. He had labored hard for breath some time, when he seemed to awake suddenly, and exclaimed, "Hark! do you hear it?"

"Hear what, my son?" asked the father.

"Their call. Look, look, at the shining ones! Oh, let me go and be at rest!"

As if waiting for this petition, the Angel of Death severed the golden thread, and he was in heaven. At midnight the messenger came.

They called Frado to see his last struggle. Sinking on her knees at the foot of his bed, she buried her face in the clothes, and wept like one inconsolable. They led her from the room. She seemed to be too much absorbed to know it was necessary for her to leave. Next day she would steal into the chamber as often as she could, to weep over his remains, and ponder his last words to her. She moved about the house like an automaton. Every duty performed — but an abstraction from all, which shewed her thoughts were busied elsewhere. Susan wished her to attend his burial as one of the family. Lewis and Mary and Jack it was not thought best to send for, as the season would not allow them time for the journey. Susan provided her with a dress for the occasion, which was her first intimation that she would be allowed to mingle her grief with others.

The day of the burial she was attired in her mourning dress; but Susan, in her grief, had forgotten a bonnet.

She hastily ransacked the closets, and found one of Mary's, trimmed with bright pink ribbon.

It was too late to change the ribbon, and she was unwilling to leave Frado at home; she knew it would be the wish of James she should go with her. So tying it on, she said, "Never mind, Frado, you shall see where our dear James is buried." As she passed out, she heard the whispers of the by-standers, "Look there! see there! how that looks, — a black dress and a pink ribbon!"

Another time, such remarks would have wounded Frado. She had now a sorrow with which such were small in comparison.

As she saw his body lowered in the grave she wished to share it; but she was not fit to die. She could not go where he was if she did. She did not love God; she did not serve him or know how to.

She retired at night to mourn over her unfitness for heaven, and gaze out upon the stars, which, she felt, studded the entrance of heaven, above which James reposed in the bosom of Jesus, to which her desires were hastening. She wished she could see God, and ask him for eternal life. Aunt Abby had taught her that He was ever looking upon her. Oh, if she could see him, or hear him speak words of forgiveness. Her anxiety increased; her health seemed impaired, and she felt constrained to go to Aunt Abby and tell her all about her conflicts.

She received her like a returning wanderer; seriously urged her to accept of Christ; explained the way; read to her from the Bible, and remarked upon such passages as applied to her state. She warned her against stifling that voice which was calling her to heaven; echoed the farewell words of James, and told her to come to her with her difficulties, and not to delay a duty so important as attention to the truths of religion, and her soul's interests.

Mrs. Bellmont would occasionally give instruction, though far different. She would tell her she could not go where James was; she need not try. If she should get to heaven at all, she would never be as high up as he.

He was the attraction. Should she "want to go there if she could not see him?"

Mrs. B. seldom mentioned her bereavement, unless in such allusion to Frado. She donned her weeds from custom; kept close her crape veil for so many Sabbaths, and abated nothing of her characteristic harshness.

The clergyman called to minister consolation to the afflicted widow and mother. Aunt Abby seeing him approach the dwelling, knew at once the object of his visit, and followed him to the parlor, unasked by Mrs. B! What a daring affront! The good man dispensed the consolations, of which he was steward, to the apparently grief-smitten mother, who talked like one schooled in a heavenly atmosphere. Such resignation expressed, as might have graced the trial of the holiest. Susan, like a mute sufferer, bared her soul to his sympathy and godly counsel, but only replied to his questions in short syllables. When he offered prayer, Frado stole to the door that she might hear of the heavenly bliss of one who was her friend on earth. The prayer caused profuse weeping, as any tender reminder of the heaven-born was sure to. When the good man's voice ceased, she returned to her toil, carefully removing all trace of sorrow. Her mistress soon followed, irritated by Nab's impudence in presenting herself unasked in the parlor, and upbraided her with indolence, and bade her apply herself more diligently. Stung by unmerited rebuke, weak from sorrow and anxiety, the tears rolled down her dark face, soon followed by sobs, and then losing all control of herself, she wept aloud. This was an act of disobedience. Her mistress grasping her raw-hide, caused a longer flow of tears, and wounded a spirit that was craving healing mercies.

CHAPTER X

Perplexities — Another Death

Neath the billows of the ocean,
Hidden treasures wait the hand,
That again to light shall raise them
With the diver's magic wand.

G. W. Cook [21]

The family, gathered by James' decease, returned to their homes. Susan and Charles returned to Baltimore. Letters were received from the absent, expressing their sympathy and grief. The father bowed like a "bruised reed," under the loss of his beloved son. He felt desirous to die the death of the righteous; also, conscious that he was unprepared, he resolved to start on the narrow way, and some time solicit entrance through the gate which leads to the celestial city. He acknowledged his too ready acquiescence with Mrs. B., in permitting Frado to be deprived of her only religious privileges for weeks together. He accordingly asked his sister to take her to meeting once more, which she was ready at once to do.

The first opportunity they once more attended meeting together. The minister conversed faithfully with every person present. He was surprised to find the little colored girl so solicitous, and kindly directed her to the flowing fountain where she might wash and be clean. He inquired of the origin of her anxiety, of her progress up to this time, and endeavored to make Christ, instead of James, the attraction of Heaven. He invited her to come to his house, to speak freely her mind to him, to pray much, to read her Bible often.

The neighbors, who were at meeting, — among them Mrs. Reed, — discussed the opinions Mrs. Bellmont would express on the subject. Mrs. Reed called and informed Mrs. B. that her colored girl "related her experience the other night at the meeting."

"What experience?" asked she, quickly, as if she expected to hear the number of times she had whipped Frado, and the number of lashes set forth in plain Arabic numbers.

"Why, you know she is serious, don't you? She told the minister about it."

Mrs. B. made no reply, but changed the subject adroitly. Next morning she told Frado she "should not go out of the house for one while, except on errands; and if she did not stop trying to be religious, she would whip her to death."

Frado pondered; her mistress was a professor of religion; was *she* going to heaven? then she did not wish to go. If she should be near James, even, she could not be happy with those fiery eyes watching her ascending path. She resolved to give over all thought of the future world, and strove daily to put her anxiety far from her.

Mr. Bellmont found himself unable to do what James or Jack could accomplish for her. He talked with her seriously, told her he had seen her many times punished undeservedly; he did not wish to have her saucy or disrespectful, but when she was *sure* she did not deserve a whipping, to avoid it if she could. "You are looking sick," he added, "you cannot endure beating as you once could."

It was not long before an opportunity offered of profiting by his advice. She was sent for wood, and not returning as soon as Mrs. B. calculated, she followed her, and, snatching from the pile a stick, raised it over her.

"Stop!" shouted Frado, "strike me, and I'll never work a mite more for you;" and throwing down what she had gathered, stood like one who feels the stirring of free and independent thoughts.

By this unexpected demonstration, her mistress, in amazement, dropped her weapon, desisting from her purpose of chastisement. Frado walked towards the house, her mistress following with the wood she herself was sent after. She did not know, before, that she had a power to ward off assaults. Her triumph in seeing her enter the door with *her* burden, repaid her for much of her former suffering.

It was characteristic of Mrs. B. never to rise in her majesty, unless she was sure she should be victorious.

This affair never met with an "after clap," like many others.

Thus passed a year. The usual amount of scolding, but fewer whippings. Mrs. B. longed once more for Mary's return, who had been absent over a year; and she wrote imperatively for her to come quickly to her. A letter came in reply, announcing that she would comply as soon as she was sufficiently recovered from an illness which detained her.

No serious apprehensions were cherished by either parent, who constantly looked for notice of her arrival, by mail. Another letter brought tidings that Mary was seriously ill; her mother's presence was solicited.

She started without delay. Before she reached her destination, a letter came to the parents announcing her death.

No sooner was the astounding news received, than Frado rushed into Aunt Abby's, exclaiming: —

"She's dead, Aunt Abby!"

"Who?" she asked, terrified by the unprefaced announcement.

"Mary; they've just had a letter."

As Mrs. B. was away, the brother and sister could freely sympathize, and she sought him in this fresh sorrow, to communicate such solace as she could, and to learn particulars of Mary's untimely death, and assist him in his journey thither.

It seemed a thanksgiving to Frado. Every hour or two she would pop in into Aunt Abby's room with some strange query:

"She got into the *river* again, Aunt Abby, didn't she; the Jordan is a big one to tumble into, any how. S'posen she goes to hell, she'll be as black as I am. Wouldn't mistress be mad to see her a nigger!" and others of a similar stamp, not at all acceptable to the pious, sympathetic dame; but she could not evade them.

The family returned from their sorrowful journey, leaving the dead behind. Nig looked for a change in her tyrant; what could subdue her, if the loss of her idol could not?

Never was Mrs. B. known to shed tears so profusely, as when she reiterated to one and another the sad particulars of her darling's sickness and death. There was, indeed, a season of quiet grief; it was the lull of the fiery elements. A few weeks revived the former tempests, and so at variance did they seem with chastisement sanctified, that Frado felt them to be unbearable. She determined to flee. But where? Who would take her? Mrs. B. had always represented her ugly. Perhaps every one thought her so. Then no one would take her. She was black, no one would love her. She might have to return, and then she would be more in her mistress' power than ever.

She remembered her victory at the wood-pile. She decided to remain to do as well as she could; to assert her rights when they were trampled on; to return once more to her meeting in the evening, which had been prohibited. She had learned how to conquer; she would not abuse the power while Mr. Bellmont was at home.

But had she not better run away? Where? She had never been from the place far enough to decide what course to take. She resolved to speak to Aunt Abby. *She* mapped the dangers of her course, her liability to fail in finding so good friends as John and herself. Frado's mind was busy for days and nights. She contemplated administering poison to her mistress, to rid herself and the house of so detestable a plague.

But she was restrained by an overruling Providence; and finally decided to stay contentedly through her period of service, which would expire when she was eighteen years of age.

In a few months Jane returned home with her family, to relieve her parents, upon whom years and affliction had left the marks of age. The years intervening since she had left her home, had, in some degree, softened the opposition to her unsanctioned marriage with George. The more Mrs. B. had about her, the more energetic seemed her directing capabilities, and her fault-finding propensities. Her own, she had full power over; and Jane after vain endeavors, became disgusted, weary, and perplexed, and decided that, though her mother might suffer, she could not endure her home. They followed Jack to the West. Thus vanished all hopes of sympathy or relief from this source to Frado. There seemed no one capable of enduring the oppressions of the house but her. She turned to the darkness of the future with the determination previously formed, to remain until she should be eighteen. Jane begged her to follow her so soon as she should be released; but so wearied out was she by her mistress, she felt disposed to flee from any and every one having her similitude of name or feature.

CHAPTER XI

Marriage Again

Crucified the hopes that cheered me,
All that to the earth endeared me;
Love of wealth and fame and power,
Love, – all have been crucified.

C. E.[22]

Darkness before day. Jane left, but Jack was now to come again. After Mary's death he visited home, leaving a wife behind. An orphan whose home was with a relative, gentle, loving, the true mate of kind, generous Jack. His mother was a stranger to her, of course, and had perfect right to interrogate:

"Is she good looking, Jack?" asked his mother.

"Looks well to me," was the laconic reply.

"Was her *father* rich?"

"Not worth a copper, as I know of; I never asked him," answered Jack.

"Hadn't she any property? What did you marry her for," asked his mother.

"Oh, she's *worth a million* dollars, mother, though not a cent of it is in money."

"Jack! what do you want to bring such a poor being into the family for? You'd better stay here, at home, and let your wife go. Why couldn't you try to do better, and not disgrace your parents?"

"Don't judge, till you see her," was Jack's reply, and immediately changed the subject. It was no recommendation to his mother, and she did not feel prepared to welcome her cordially now he was to come with his wife. He was indignant at his mother's advice to desert her. It rankled bitterly in his soul, the bare suggestion. He had more to bring. He now came with a child also. He decided to leave the West, but not his family.

Upon their arrival, Mrs. B. extended a cold welcome to her new daughter, eyeing her dress with closest scrutiny. Poverty was to her a disgrace, and she could not associate with any thus dishonored. This coldness was felt by Jack's worthy wife, who only strove the harder to recommend herself by her obliging, winning ways.

Mrs. B. could never let Jack be with her alone without complaining of this or that deficiency in his wife.

He cared not so long as the complaints were piercing his own ears. He would not have Jenny disquieted. He passed his time in seeking employment.

A letter came from his brother Lewis, then at the South, soliciting his services. Leaving his wife, he repaired thither.

Mrs. B. felt that great restraint was removed, that Jenny was more in her own power. She wished to make her feel her inferiority; to relieve Jack of his burden if he would not do it himself. She watched her incessantly, to catch at some act of Jenny's which might be construed into conjugal unfaithfulness.

Near by were a family of cousins, one a young man of Jack's age, who, from love to his cousin, proffered all needful courtesy to his stranger relative. Soon news reached Jack that Jenny was deserting her covenant vows, and had formed an illegal intimacy with his cousin. Meantime Jenny was told by her mother-in-law that Jack did not marry her untrammelled. He had another love whom he would be glad, even now, if he could, to marry. It was very doubtful if he ever came for her.

Jenny would feel pained by her unwelcome gossip, and, glancing at her child, she decided, however true it might be, she had a pledge which would enchain him yet. Ere long, the mother's inveterate hate crept out into some neighbor's enclosure, and, caught up hastily, they passed the secret round till it became none, and Lewis was sent for, the brother by whom Jack was employed. The neighbors saw her fade in health and spirits; they found letters never reached their destination when sent by either. Lewis arrived with the joyful news that he had come to take Jenny home with him.

What a relief to her to be freed from the gnawing taunts of her adversary.

Jenny retired to prepare for the journey, and Mrs. B. and Henry[23] had a long interview. Next morning he informed Jenny that new clothes would be necessary, in order to make her presentable to Baltimore society, and he should return without her, and she must stay till she was suitably attired.

Disheartened, she rushed to her room, and, after relief from weeping, wrote to Jack to come; to have pity on her, and take her to him. No answer came. Mrs. Smith, a neighbor, watchful and friendly, suggested that she write away from home, and employ some one to carry it to the office who would elude Mrs. B., who, they very well knew, had intercepted Jenny's letter, and influenced Lewis to leave her behind. She accepted the offer, and Frado succeeded in managing the affair so that Jack soon came to the rescue, angry, wounded, and forever after alienated from his early home and his mother. Many times would Frado steal up into Jenny's room, when she knew she was tortured by her mistress' malignity, and tell some of her own encounters with her, and tell her she might "be sure it wouldn't kill her, for she should have died long before at the same treatment."

Susan and her child succeeded Jenny as visitors. Frado had merged into womanhood, and, retaining what she had learned, in spite of the few privileges enjoyed formerly, was striving to enrich her mind. Her school-books were her constant companions, and every leisure moment was applied to them. Susan was delighted to witness her progress, and some little book from her was a reward sufficient for any task imposed, however difficult. She had her book always fastened open near her, where she could glance from toil to soul refreshment. The approaching spring would close the term of years which Mrs. B. claimed as the period of her servitude. Often as she passed the way-marks of former years did she pause to ponder on her situation, and wonder if she *could* succeed in providing for her own wants. Her health was delicate, yet she resolved to try.

Soon she counted the time by days which should release her. Mrs. B. felt that she could not well spare one who could so well adapt herself to all departments – man, boy, housekeeper, domestic, etc. She begged Mrs. Smith to talk with her, to show her how ungrateful it would appear to leave a home of such comfort – how wicked it was to be ungrateful! But Frado replied that she had had enough of such comforts; she wanted some new ones; and as it was so wicked to be ungrateful, she would go from temptation; Aunt Abby said "we mustn't put ourselves in the way of temptation."

Poor little Fido! She shed more tears over him than over all beside.

The morning for departure dawned. Frado engaged to work for a family a mile distant. Mrs. Bellmont dismissed her with the assurance that she would soon wish herself back again, and a present of a silver half dollar.

Her wardrobe consisted of one decent dress, without any superfluous accompaniments. A Bible from Susan she felt was her greatest treasure.

Now was she alone in the world. The past year had been one of suffering resulting from a fall, which had left her lame.

The first summer passed pleasantly, and the wages earned were expended in garments necessary for health and cleanliness. Though feeble, she was well satisfied with her progress. Shut up in her room, after her toil was finished, she studied what poor samples of apparel she had, and, for the first time, prepared her own garments.

Mrs. Moore, who employed her, was a kind friend to her, and attempted to heal her wounded spirit by sympathy and advice, burying the past in the prospects of the future. But her failing health was a cloud no kindly human hand could dissipate. A little light work was all she could accomplish. A clergyman, whose family was small, sought her, and she was removed there. Her engagement with Mrs. Moore finished in the fall. Frado was anxious to keep up her reputation for efficiency, and often pressed far beyond prudence. In the winter she entirely gave up work, and confessed herself thoroughly sick. Mrs. Hale, soon overcome by additional cares, was taken sick also, and now it became necessary to adopt some measures for Frado's comfort, as well as to relieve Mrs. Hale. Such dark forebodings as visited her as she lay, solitary and sad, no moans or sighs could relieve.

The family physician pronounced her case one of doubtful issue. Frado hoped it was final. She could not feel relentings that her former home was abandoned, and yet, should she be in need of succor could she obtain it from one who would now so grudgingly bestow it? The family were applied to, and it was decided to take her there. She was removed to a room built out from the main building, used formerly as a workshop, where cold and rain found unobstructed access, and here she fought with bitter reminiscences and future prospects till she became reckless of her faith and hopes and person, and half wished to end what nature seemed so tardily to take.

Aunt Abby made her frequent visits, and at last had her removed to her own apartment, where she might supply her wants, and minister to her once more in heavenly things.

Then came the family consultation.

"What is to be done with her," asked Mrs. B., "after she is moved there with Nab?"

"Send for the Dr., your brother," Mr. B. replied.

"When?"

"To-night."

"To-night! and for her! Wait till morning," she continued.

"She has waited too long now; I think some thing should be done soon."

"I doubt if she is much sick," sharply interrupted Mrs. B.

"Well, we'll see what our brother thinks."

His coming was longed for by Frado, who had known him well during her long sojourn in the family; and his praise of her nice butter and cheese, from which his table was supplied, she knew he felt as well as spoke.

"You're sick, very sick," he said, quickly, after a moment's pause. "Take good care of her, Abby, or she'll never get well. All broken down."

"Yes, it was at Mrs. Moore's," said Mrs. B., "all this was done. She did but little the latter part of the time she was here."

"It was commenced longer ago than last summer. Take good care of her; she may never get well," remarked the Dr.

"We sha'n't pay you for doctoring her; you may look to the town for that, sir," said Mrs. B., and abruptly left the room.

"Oh dear! oh dear!" exclaimed Frado, and buried her face in the pillow.

A few kind words of consolation, and she was once more alone in the darkness which enveloped her previous days. Yet she felt sure they owed her a shelter and attention, when disabled, and she resolved to feel patient, and remain till she could help herself. Mrs. B. would not attend her, nor permit her domestic to stay with her at all. Aunt Abby was her sole comforter. Aunt Abby's nursing had the desired effect, and she slowly improved. As soon as she was able to be moved, the kind Mrs. Moore took her to her home again, and completed what Aunt Abby had so well commenced. Not that she was well, or ever would be; but she had recovered so far as rendered it hopeful she might provide for her own wants. The clergyman at whose house she was taken sick, was now seeking some one to watch his sick children, and as soon as he heard of her recovery, again asked for her services.

What seemed so light and easy to others, was too much for Frado; and it became necessary to ask once more where the sick should find an asylum.

All felt that the place where her declining health began, should be the place of relief; so they applied once more for a shelter.

"No," exclaimed the indignant Mrs. B.; "she shall never come under this roof again; never! never!" she repeated, as if each repetition were a bolt to prevent admission.

One only resource; the public must pay the expense. So she was removed to the home of two maidens, (old,) who had principle enough to be willing to earn the money a charitable public disburses.

Three years of weary sickness wasted her, without extinguishing a life apparently so feeble. Two years had these maidens watched and cared for her, and they began to weary, and finally to request the authorities to remove her.

Mrs. Hoggs was a lover of gold and silver, and she asked the favor of filling her coffers by caring for the sick. The removal caused severe sickness.

By being bolstered in the bed, after a time she could use her hands, and often would ask for sewing to beguile the tedium. She had become very expert with her needle the first year of her release from Mrs. B., and she had forgotten none of her skill. Mrs. H. praised her, and as she improved in health, was anxious to employ her. She told her she could in this way replace her clothes, and as her board would be paid for, she would thus gain something.

Many times her hands wrought when her body was in pain; but the hope that she might yet help herself, impelled her on.

Thus she reckoned her store of means by a few dollars, and was hoping soon to come in possession, when she was startled by the announcement that Mrs. Hoggs had reported her to the physician and town officers as an impostor. That she was, in truth, able to get up and go to work.

This brought on a severe sickness of two weeks, when Mrs. Moore again sought her, and took her to her home. She had formerly had wealth at her command, but misfortune had deprived her of it, and unlocked her heart to sympathies and favors she had never known while it lasted. Her husband, defrauded of his last means by a branch of the Bellmont family, had supported them by manual labor, gone to the West, and left his wife and four young children. But she felt humanity required her to give a shelter to one she knew to be worthy of a hospitable reception. Mrs. Moore's physician was called, and pronounced her a very sick girl, and encouraged Mrs. M. to keep her and care for her, and he would see that the authorities were informed of Frado's helplessness, and pledged assistance.

Here she remained till sufficiently restored to sew again. Then came the old resolution to take care of herself, to cast off the unpleasant charities of the public.

She learned that in some towns in Massachusetts, girls make straw bonnets – that it was easy and profitable. But how should *she*, black, feeble and poor, find any one to teach her. But God prepares the way, when human agencies see no path. Here was found a plain, poor, simple woman, who could see merit beneath a dark skin; and when the invalid mulatto told her sorrows, she opened her door and her heart, and took the stranger in. Expert with the needle, Frado soon equalled her instructress; and she sought also to teach her the value of useful books; and while one read aloud to the other of deeds historic and names renowned, Frado experienced a new impulse. She felt herself capable of elevation; she felt that this book information supplied an undefined dissatisfaction she had long felt, but could not express. Every leisure moment was carefully applied to self-improvement, and a devout and Christian exterior invited confidence from the villagers. Thus she passed months of quiet, growing in the confidence of her neighbors and new found friends.

CHAPTER XII

The Winding Up of the Matter

Nothing new under the sun.

Solomon [24]

A few years ago, within the compass of my narrative, there appeared often in some of our New England villages, professed fugitives from slavery,[25] who recounted their personal experience in homely phrase, and awakened the indignation of non-slaveholders against brother Pro.[26] Such a one appeared in the new home of Frado; and as people of color were rare there, was it strange she should attract her dark brother; that he should inquire her out; succeed in seeing her; feel a strange sensation in his heart towards her; that he should toy with her shining curls, feel proud to provoke her to smile and expose the ivory concealed by thin, ruby lips; that her sparkling eyes should fascinate; that he should propose; that they should marry? A short acquaintance was indeed an objection, but she saw him often, and thought she knew him. He never spoke of his enslavement to her when alone, but she felt that, like her own oppression, it was painful to disturb oftener than was needful.

He was a fine, straight negro, whose back showed no marks of the lash, erect as if it never crouched beneath a burden. There was a silent sympathy which Frado felt attracted her, and she opened her heart to the presence of love – that arbitrary and inexorable tyrant.

She removed to Singleton, her former residence, and there was married. Here were Frado's first feelings of trust and repose on human arm. She realized, for the first time, the relief of looking to another for comfortable support. Occasionally he would leave her to "lecture."

Those tours were prolonged often to weeks. Of course he had little spare money. Frado was again feeling her self-dependence, and was at last compelled to resort alone to that. Samuel was kind to her when at home, but made no provision for his absence, which was at last unprecedented.

He left her to her fate — embarked at sea, with the disclosure that he had never seen the South, and that his illiterate harangues were humbugs for hungry abolitionists.[27] Once more alone! Yet not alone. A still newer companionship would soon force itself upon her. No one wanted her with such prospects. Herself was burden enough; who would have an additional one?

The horrors of her condition nearly prostrated her, and she was again thrown upon the public for sustenance. Then followed the birth of her child. The long absent Samuel unexpectedly returned, and rescued her from charity. Recovering from her expected illness, she once more commenced toil for herself and child, in a room obtained of a poor woman, but with better fortune. One so well known would not be wholly neglected. Kind friends watched her when Samuel was from home, prevented her from suffering, and when the cold weather pinched the warmly clad, a kind friend took them in, and thus preserved them. At last Samuel's business became very engrossing, and after long desertion, news reached his family that he had become a victim of yellow fever, in New Orleans.

So much toil as was necessary to sustain Frado, was more than she could endure. As soon as her babe could be nourished without his mother, she left him in charge of a Mrs. Capon, and procured an agency, hoping to recruit her health, and gain an easier livelihood for herself and child. This afforded her better maintenance than she had yet found. She passed into the various towns of the State she lived in, then into Massachusetts. Strange were some of her adventures. Watched by kidnappers, maltreated by professed abolitionists, who didn't want slaves at the South, nor niggers in their own houses, North.[28] Faugh! to lodge one; to eat with one; to admit one through the front door;

to sit next one; awful![29]

Traps slyly laid by the vicious to ensnare her,[30] she resolutely avoided. In one of her tours, Providence favored her with a friend who, pitying her cheerless lot, kindly provided her with a valuable recipe, from which she might herself manufacture a useful article for her maintenance. This proved a more agreeable, and an easier way of sustenance.

And thus, to the present time, may you see her busily employed in preparing her merchandise; then sallying forth to encounter many frowns, but some kind friends and purchasers. Nothing turns her from her steadfast purpose of elevating herself. Reposing on God, she has thus far journeyed securely. Still an invalid, she asks your sympathy, gentle reader. Refuse not, because some part of her history is unknown, save by the Omniscient God. Enough has been unrolled to demand your sympathy and aid.

Do you ask the destiny of those connected with her *early* history? A few years only have elapsed since Mr. and Mrs. B. passed into another world. As age increased, Mrs. B. became more irritable, so that no one, even her own children, could remain with her; and she was accompanied by her husband to the home of Lewis, where, after an agony in death unspeakable, she passed away. Only a few months since, Aunt Abby entered heaven. Jack and his wife rest in heaven, disturbed by no intruders; and Susan and her child are yet with the living. Jane has silver locks in place of auburn tresses, but she has the early love of Henry still, and has never regretted her exchange of lovers. Frado has passed from their memories, as Joseph from the butler's,[31] but she will never cease to track them till beyond mortal vision.

Appendix [32]

"TRUTH is stranger than fiction;" and whoever reads the narrative of Alfrado, will find the assertion verified.

About eight years ago I became acquainted with the author of this book, and I feel it a privilege to speak a few words in her behalf. Through the instrumentality of an itinerant colored lecturer, she was brought to W_____, Mass. This is an ancient town, where the mothers and daughters seek, not "wool and flax," but *straw*, – working willingly with their hands! Here she was introduced to the family of Mrs. Walker, who kindly consented to receive her as an inmate of her household, and immediately succeeded in procuring work for her as a "straw sewer." Being very ingenious, she soon acquired the art of making hats; but on account of former hard treatment, her constitution was greatly impaired, and she was subject to seasons of sickness. On this account Mrs. W. gave her a room joining her own chamber, where she could hear her faintest call. Never shall I forget the expression of her "black, but comely" face, as she came to me one day, exclaiming, "O, aunt J_____, I have at last found a *home*, – and not only a home, but a *mother*. My cup runneth over. What shall I render to the Lord for all his benefits?" [33]

Months passed on, and she was *happy* – truly happy. Her health began to improve under the genial sunshine in which she lived, and she even looked forward with *hope* – joyful hope to the future. But, alas, "it is not in man that walketh to direct his steps." [34] One beautiful morning in the early spring of 1842, as she was taking her usual walk, she chanced to meet her old friend, the "lecturer," who brought her to W_____, and with him was a fugitive slave. Young, well-formed and very handsome, he said he had been a *house*-servant, which seemed to account in some measure for his gentlemanly manners and pleasing address. The meeting was entirely accidental; but it was a sad occurrence for poor Alfrado, as her own sequel tells. Suffice it to say, an acquaintance and attachment was formed, which, in due time, resulted in marriage. In a few days she left W_____, and *all* her home comforts, and took up her abode in New Hampshire. For a while everything went on well, and she dreamed not of danger; but in an evil hour he left his young and trusting wife, and embarked for sea. She knew nothing of all this, and waited for his return. But she waited in vain. Days passed, weeks passed, and he came not; then her heart failed her. She felt herself deserted at a time, when, of all others, she most needed the care and soothing attentions of a devoted husband. For a time she tried to sustain *herself,* but this was impossible. She had friends, but they were mostly of that class who are poor in the things of earth, but "rich in faith." [35] The charity on which she depended failed at last, and there was nothing to save her from the "County House;" *go she must.* But her feelings on her way thither, and after her arrival, can be given better in her own language; and I trust it will be no breach of confidence if I here insert part of a letter she wrote her mother Walker, concerning the matter.

*   *   *

"The evening before I left for my dreaded journey to the 'house' which was to be my abode, I packed my trunk, carefully placing in it every little memento of affection received from *you* and my friends in W_____, among which was the portable inkstand, pens and paper. My beautiful little Bible was laid aside, as a place nearer my heart was reserved for that. I need not tell you I slept not a moment that night. My home, my peaceful, quiet home with you, was before me. I could see my dear little room, with its pleasant eastern window opening to the morning; but more than all, I beheld *you,* my mother, gliding softly in and kneeling by my bed to read, as no one but you *can* read, 'The Lord is my shepherd, – I shall not want.' [36] But I cannot go on, for tears blind me. For a description of the morning, and of the scant breakfast, I must wait until another time.

"We started. The man who came for me was kind as he could be, – helped me carefully into the wagon, (for I had no strength,) and drove on. For miles I spoke not a word. Then the silence would be broken by the driver uttering some sort of word the horse seemed to understand; for he invariably quickened his pace. And so, just before nightfall, we halted at the institution, prepared for the *homeless*. With cold civility the matron received me, and bade one of the inmates shew me my room. She did so; and I followed up two flights of stairs. I crept as I was able; and when she said, 'Go in there,' I obeyed, asking for my trunk, which was soon placed by me. My room was furnished some like the 'prophet's chamber,' except there was no 'candlestick;' so when I could creep down I begged for a light, and it was granted. Then I flung myself on the bed and cried, until I could cry no longer. I rose up and tried to pray; the Saviour seemed near. I opened my precious little Bible, and the first verse that caught my eye was – 'I am poor and needy, yet the Lord thinketh upon me.'[37] O, my mother, could I tell you the comfort this was to me. I sat down, calm, almost happy, took my pen and wrote on the inspiration of the moment –

"O, holy Father, by thy power,
   Thus far in life I'm brought;
And now in this dark, trying hour,
   O God, forsake me not.

"Dids't thou not nourish and sustain
   My infancy and youth?
Have I not testimonials plain,
   Of thy unchanging truth?

"Though I've no home to call my own,
   My heart shall not repine;
The saint may live on earth unknown,
   And yet in glory shine.

"When my Redeemer dwelt below,
 He chose a lowly lot;
He came unto his own, but lo!
 His own received him not.

"Oft was the mountain his abode,
 The cold, cold earth his bed;
The midnight moon shone softly down
 On his unsheltered head.[37]

"But *my* head *was sheltered,* and I tried to feel thankful."

* * *

TWO or three letters were received after this by her friends in
W_____ , and then all was silent. No one of us knew whether she
still lived or had gone to her home on high. But it seems she remained
in this house until after the birth of her babe; then her faithless husband
returned, and took her to some town in New Hampshire, where, for
a time, he supported her and his little son decently well. But again he
left her as before – suddenly and unexpectedly, and she saw him no
more. Her efforts were again successful in a measure in securing a
meagre maintenance for a time; but her struggles with poverty and
sickness were severe. At length, a door of hope was opened. A kind
gentleman and lady took her little boy into their own family, and
provided everything neccessary for his good; and all this without the
hope of remuneration. But let them know, they shall be "recompensed
at the resurrection of the just." [39] God is not unmindful of this work,
– this labor of love. As for the afflicted mother, she too has been
remembered. The heart of a stranger was moved with compassion, and
bestowed a recipe upon her for restoring gray hair to its former color.
She availed herself of this great help, and has been quite successful;
but her health is again falling, and she has felt herself obliged to resort

to another method of procuring her bread — that of writing an Autobiography.

I trust she will find a ready sale for her interesting work; and let all the friends who purchase a volume, remember they are doing good to one of the most worthy, and I had almost said most unfortunate, of the human family. I will only add in conclusion, a few lines, calculated to comfort and strengthen this sorrowful, homeless one. "I will help thee, saith the Lord." [40]

"I will help thee," promise kind,
   Made by our High Priest above;
Soothing to the troubled mind,
   Full of tenderness and love.

"I will help thee" when the storm
   Gathers dark on every side;
Safely from impending harm,
   In my sheltering bosom hide

"I will help thee," weary saint,
   Cast thy burdens *all on me*;
Oh, how cans't thou tire or faint,
   While my arm encircles thee.

I have pitied every tear,
   Heard and *counted* every sigh;
Ever lend a gracious ear
   To thy supplicating cry.

What though thy wounded bosom bleed,
   Pierced by affliction's dart;
Do I not all thy sorrows heed,
   And bear thee on my heart?

Soon will the lowly grave become
   Thy quiet resting place;
Thy spirit find a peaceful home
   In mansions *near my face.*

There are thy robes and glittering crown,
   Outshining yonder sun;
Soon shalt thou lay the body down,
   And put those glories on.

Long has thy golden lyre been strung,
   Which angels cannot move;
No song to this is ever sung,
   But bleeding, dying Love.[41]

ALLIDA[42]

*   *   *

TO THE FRIENDS OF OUR DARK-COMPLEXIONED BRETHREN AND SISTERS,
THIS NOTE IS INTENDED.

Having known the writer of this book for a number of years, and
knowing the many privations and mortifications she has had to pass
through, I the more willingly add my testimony to the truth of her
assertions. She is one of that class, who by some are considered not
only as little lower than the angels, but far beneath them; but I have
long since learned that we are not to look at the color of the hair, the
eyes, or the skin, for the man or woman; their life is the criterion we
are to judge by. The writer of this book has seemed to be a child of
misfortune.

Early in life she was deprived of her parents, and all those endearing
associations to which childhood clings. Indeed, she may be said to have
had that happy period; for, being taken from home so young, and
placed where she had nothing to love or cling to, I often wonder she

had not grown up a *monster*; and those very people calling themselves Christians, (the good Lord deliver me from such,) and they likewise ruined her health by hard work, both in the field and house. She was indeed a slave, in every sense of the word; and a lonely one, too.

But she has found some friends in this degraded world, that were willing to do by others as they would have others do by them; that were willing she should live, and have an existence on the earth with them. She has never enjoyed any degree of comfortable health since she was eighteen years of age, and a great deal of the time has been confined to her room and bed. She is now trying to write a book; and I hope the public will look favorably on it, and patronize the same, for she is a worthy woman.

Her own health being poor, and having a child to care for, (for, by the way, she has been married,) and she wishes to educate him; in her sickness he has been taken from her, and sent to the country farm, because she could not pay his board every week; but as soon as she was able, she took him from that *place*, and now he has a home where he is contented and happy, and where he is considered as good as those he is with. He is an intelligent, smart boy, and no doubt will make a smart man, if he is rightly managed. He is beloved by his playmates, and by all the friends of the family; for the family do not recognize those as friends who do not include him in their family, or as one of them, and his mother as a daughter – for they treat her as such; and she certainly deserves all the affection and kindness that is bestowed upon her, and they are always happy to have her visit them whenever she will. They are not wealthy, but the latch-string is always out when suffering humanity needs a shelter; the last loaf they are willing to divide with those more needy than themselves, remembering these words, Do good as we have opportunity; and we can always find opportunity, if we have the disposition.[43]

And now I would say, I hope those who call themselves friends of our dark-skinned brethren, will lend a helping hand, and assist our sister, not in giving, but in buying a book; the expense is trifling, and the reward of doing good is great. Our duty is to our fellow-beings, and when we let an opportunity pass, we know not what we lose. Therefore we should do with all our might what our hands find to do; and remember the words of Him who went about doing good, that inasmuch as ye have done a good deed to one of the least of these my brethren, ye have done it to me;[44] and even a cup of water is not forgotten. Therefore, let us work while the day lasts, and we shall in no wise lose our reward.

MARGARETTA THORN.[45]

*   *   *

MILFORD,[46] JULY 20th, 1859.

Feeling a deep interest in the welfare of the writer of this book, and hoping that its circulation will be extensive, I wish to say a few words in her behalf. I have been acquainted with her for several years, and have always found her worthy the esteem of all friends of humanity; one whose soul is alive to the work to which she puts her hand. Although her complexion is a little darker than my own, I esteem it a privilege to associate with her, and assist her whenever an opportunity presents itself. It is with this motive that I write these few lines, knowing this book must be interesting to all who have any knowledge of the writer's character, or wish to have. I hope no one will refuse to aid her in her work, as she is worthy the sympathy of all Christians, and those who have a spark of humanity in their breasts.

Thinking it unneccessary for me to write a long epistle, I will close by bidding her God speed.

C. D. S.[47]

NOTES

The Notes to this edition are divided into two sections. The first set of notes, which are numbered footnotes, consists chiefly of expository observations. The second set of notes (which give page and line references) includes indications where the original text has been altered to remove printer's errors or inconsistencies. These changes are designed to make this edition read more easily, and have been left silent in the text.

Footnotes

Title Page

The quotation on the title page occurs in Josiah Gilbert Holland, *Bitter-Sweet: A Poem*. In the 5th ed. of *Bitter-Sweet* (N.Y.: Charles Scribner, 1859) these lines appear on pp. 35-36. Wilson's quotation is largely, but not wholly, accurate. The quotation in the 1859 edition reads:

I know

That care has iron crowns for many brows;
That Calvaries are everywhere, whereon
Virtue is crucified, and nails and spears
Draw guiltless blood; that sorrow sits and drinks
At sweetest hearts, till all their life is dry;
That gentle spirits on the rack of pain
Grow faint or fierce, and pray and curse by turns;
That Hell's temptations, clad in Heavenly guise
And armed with might, lie evermore in wait
Along life's path, giving assault to all –

The quotation occurs in the twenty-second speech of the 'First Movement', spoken by 'Ruth'. The next two lines continue: 'I know the world is full of evil things,/ And shudder with the consciousness.' This is a repeated pattern in *Our Nig*: the quotes selected, presumably by Wilson, are in themselves apposite, but also, almost without exception, the contexts from which the quotations are taken add further pertinence. This would seem to indicate that she was well-read, and lends weight to an interpretation of the text regarding it as a sophisticated narrative, fully capable of complex moments of reflexivity and meta-textuality.

PREFACE

1. Wilson here seems to indicate that her novel was aimed at a 'colored' audience. However, the copies of *Our Nig* that have survived seem to have been owned by white Americans, including the son of the abolitionist leader, William Lloyd Garrison. See Eric Gardner's research (Gardner, 1993, passim). Perhaps Wilson is not so much indicating that she expects her readership to be black but rather that only African Americans will be prepared fully to attend to her message concerning the prevalence of racism in the 'two-story' North or be moved sufficiently to lend her financial or other material support. I am, however, not sure that the text does solely orientate itself to a 'colored' readership, and my doubts are fuelled by the 'Preface' itself: why should Wilson 'purposely omit' from her novel 'what would most provoke shame in our good anti-slavery friends at home' if she did not expect at least some white readers?

2. The initials H. E. W. correspond to those in the name Mrs. H. E. Wilson, by whom the book was copyrighted. The copyright page of the original 1859 edition read: 'Entered according to Act of of Congress, in the year 1859,/ BY MRS. H. E. WILSON,/ In the Clerk's office of the District Court of the District of Massachusetts'. The way the initials appended to the preface correspond to the name of the individual claiming copyright proved to be a key part of the means by which the author behind the pseudonym "Our Nig" became identifiable.

Chapter I

3. (p. 1). The use of first-person pronominals in the titles of the first three chapters does not meld with the third-person narrative voice. The use of 'my' and 'me' might suggest an autobiographical

intention. Alternatively, it might be regarded as a device to dramatise the human dilemma of Frado – by personalising her, giving her a voice.

4. (p. 1). The quotation is taken from Thomas Moore, 'Lalla Rookh'. It can be found in *The Poetical Works of Thomas Moore, Collected by Himself*, Philadelphia: J. B. Lippencott, 1858, p. 257. Wilson's quotation is not wholly accurate. The version in the 1858 edition reads:

> Oh, Grief, beyond all other griefs, when fate
> First leaves the young heart alone and desolate
> In the wide world, without that only tie
> For which it lov'd to live or fear'd to die; –
> Lorn as the hung-up lute, that ne'er hath spoken
> Since the sad day its master-chord was broken!

Chapter II

5. (p. 6). The quotation is taken from Percy Bysshe Shelley, 'Misery – A Fragment'. This can be found in *The Poetical Works of Percy Bysshe Shelley*, edited by Mrs. Shelley, with a memoir, New York: Little, Brown and Co., 1835, vol. 2, p. 399. Wilson's quotation is not quite accurate. The quotation in the 1835 edition reads:

> Misery! we have known each other,
> Like a sister and a brother
> Living in the same lone home,
> Many years – we must live some
> Hours or ages yet to come.

The quotation is made up of stanza 3. Stanza 4 commences: ''Tis an evil lot, and yet/ Let us make the best of it'.

6. (p. 7). This is the only point in the book where Frado is described as beautiful (though p. 6 mentions 'two pretty mulattos' and on p. 7 Seth describes Frado as '"six years old, and pretty"'). It is also one

of only five places where her skin colour is drawn to the reader's attention. Beside p. 6's passing mention of her as a mulatto, on p. 9 we are told she is "'yeller'" and on p. 12 that she is "'not very black'". More discursively, on p. 19, the text describes Mrs. B.'s determination to keep Frado in the sun to ensure her skin darkens, to help distinguish Frado from Mary Bellmont. This comparative reticence about Frado's beauty and hue militates against viewing *Our Nig* as just another sentimental fiction focusing on a 'tragic octoroon'. Her story breaks the pattern. Thus, though Pete's lingering over 'the pleasing contrast between her [Mag's] fair face and his own dark skin' points to the terrain of gender, race and sexuality cogently, this line of enquiry is subordinate to Wilson's more immediate concern: to focus on the interaction of race, class and sadism – though this, of course, in turn, may bear within itself a loaded erotic charge. The 'dangerous passion' of Mrs. B. mentioned in Chapter VIII (p. 44) hints at how focusing on females' mistreatment of a female carries this different sort of (homoerotic) charge – one far more complex than that which the usual (stereotypical) generic emphasis on miscegenation generates.

7. (p. 9). The schoolchildren's cry provides the only way that the reader can establish that Seth Shipley is black.

Chapter III

8. (p. 11). The quotation is taken from Eliza Cook, 'The Future'. The lines can be found in *The Poetical Works of Eliza Cook*, London: Frederick Warne and Co.; New York: Scribner, Welford and Co., 1870, p. 187. Wilson's quotation is slightly inaccurate. The quotation in the 1870 edition reads:

> Oh! did we but know of the shadows so nigh,
>> The world would indeed be a prison of gloom;
> All light would be quenched in youth's eloquent eye,
>> And the prayer-lisping infant would ask for the tomb.

For if Hope be a star that may lead us astray,
  And "deceiveth the heart," as the aged ones preach;
Yet 'twas Mercy that gave it, to beacon our way,
  Though its halo illumes where we never can reach.

The quotation consists of the fourth and fifth stanzas of the poem. Stanza six runs: 'Though Friendship but flit, like a meteor gleam,/ Though it burst, like a moon-lighted bubble of dew;/ Though it passes away, like a leaf on a stream,/ Yet 'tis bliss while we *fancy* the vision is true.' These sentiments are particularly appropriate to Frado's condition in the Bellmont family, since her 'friends' in the family all repeatedly fail her.

Chapter IV

9. (p. 20). The quotation is taken from Lord Byron, 'Childish Recollections'. This can be found in *Hours of Idleness: A Series of Poems, Original and Translated* in *The Poetical Works of Lord Byron: Embracing His Suppressed Poems, and a Sketch of His Life*, London: John Murray, 1845, p. 405. Wilson's quotation is again slightly inaccurate. The quotation in the 1845 edition reads:

Hours of my youth! when, nurtured in my breast,
To love a stranger, friendship made me blest; −
Friendship, the dear peculiar bond of youth,
When every artless bosom throbs with truth;
Untaught by worldly wisdom how to feign,
And check each impulse with prudential reign;
When all we feel our honest souls disclose −
In love to friends, in open hate to foes;
No varnish'd tales the lips of youth repeat,
No dear-bought knowledge purchased by deceit.

This comes from the second stanza. The poem continues: 'Hypocrisy, the gift of lengthen'd years,/ Matured by age, the garb of prudence wears.' I take this to be a barbed reference to the shortcomings Wilson perceives in 'professed abolitionists' (p. 69).

Chapter V

10. (p. 27). This quotation comes from Martin Farquhar Tupper, 'Of Life', the second section of Tupper's 'Proverbial Philosophy'. This can be found in *Tupper's Complete Poetical Works*, Boston: Phillips, Sampson and Company, 1850, p. 192. The lines occur in the final stanza. Wilson's quotation contains some minor punctuation differences from this 1850 edition, which reads:

> Life is a strange avenue of various trees and flowers;
> Lightsome at commencement, but darkening to its end in a
>   distant, massy portal.
> It beginneth as a little path, edged with the violet and primrose,
> A little path of lawny grass, and soft to tiny feet:
> Soon, spring thistles in the way, ...

This final stanza from 'Of Life' continues, appositely: 'Soon, spring thistles in the way, those early griefs of school,/ And fruit trees ranged on either hand show holiday delights:/ Anon, the rose and the mimosa hint at sensitive affection,/ And vipers hide among the grass, and briers are woven in the hedges'.

Chapter VI

11. (p. 33). The quotation is taken from Laetitia Elizabeth Landon, 'Success Alone Seen'. This can be found in *Life and Literary Remains of L. E. L.*, by Laman Blanchard, London: Henry Colburn, 1841, p. 261. The passage has been reproduced as prose, and slightly inaccurately; the quotation in the 1841 edition reads:

> Hard are life's early steps; and, but that youth
> Is buoyant, confident, and strong in hope,
> Men would behold its threshold and despair.

12. (p. 33). This estimation of the dog as more valuable to Frado than the human beings around her represents the climax of the ironic Frado/Fido motif which began in Chapter III (p. 17).

13. (p. 34). The recurrence of essentially novelistic moments of omniscient narration, like this insight into Mary's 'mental vision', weigh powerfully against viewing the text as an autobiography.

Chapter VII

14. (p. 39). The quotation is taken from Henry Kirke White, 'Time: A Poem'. This appears in *The poetical works of Henry Kirke White*, London: Bell and Daldy, 1830, p. 20. The quotation comes from the fourth stanza.

Chapter VIII

15. (p. 42). The quotation is taken from Henry Kirke White, 'Written in the Prospect of Death'. This appears in *The poetical works of Henry Kirke White*, London: Bell and Daldy, 1830, p. 79. Wilson's quotation has some inaccuracies. In this 1830 edition the lines read:

> Now other cares engross me,
> And my tired soul with emulative haste,
> Looks to its God.

The lines immediately preceding this quote read: 'No more of Hope; the wanton vagrant Hope!/ I abjure all.' This was evidently a favourite poem of Wilson's, as she also quotes from it at the head of Chapter IX.

16. (p. 45). One of the more remarkable features of this novel is its failure to conform closely to the predominant convention existing in contemporary slave narratives or other writings by African Americans: that a conversion narrative be incorporated, in which the African American hero arrives at Christ. From this point in Wilson's novel, as Frado doubts if African Americans have a place in the Christian heaven, to the end of the text, what is on offer instead of

any sure conversion is an uneasy oscillation, as Frado approaches but, finally, never fully embraces the Church. She is seen to be 'serious', but never sheds her doubts about what the Christian Church truly offers to African Americans. Given the predominance of the conversion narrative model that *Our Nig* at best only half matches, the uneasiness that instead prevails can be seen as subversive indeed.

17. (p. 48). Frado appears to be a species of indentured servant, and the general assumption by critics is that the Bellmonts were paid for looking after her, so taking her off the hands of the town of Singleton, which would otherwise need to support her until she came of age. The suggestion here that the Bellmonts have to 'beat the money out of' Frado to get her 'worth' seems not to support such a reading. Rather, on the face of it, what seems to be implied is that either the Bellmonts pay the town for her services or, more brutally, that, since slavery is abolished in the North, and so she cannot now be sold as a slave for profit, she must work to earn her value, which would be lost to the Bellmonts otherwise. This speech by Mrs. B. therefore offers further support for the proposition that to regard *Our Nig* as autobiography is an over-facile option, since Barbara A. White (White, 1993, p. 34) believes that the Hayward family who abused Harriet Wilson in Milford in fact received public money to pay for her upkeep. (This makes it more difficult for critics who equate Frado's position with Wilson's, given what the text seems to indicate here.) Wilson's adjustment to history surely creates an effective dramatisation of the economic issues at the heart of this text.

18. (p. 48). Luke, 18, xiii: 'And the publican, standing afar off, would not lift up so much as his eyes unto heaven, but smote upon his breast, saying, God be merciful to me a sinner.' The oblique allusion is both to Frado's downcast eyes and to the fact that 'he that humblest himself shall be exalted' (Luke, 18, xiv).

Chapter IX

19. (p. 49). The quotation is taken from Henry Kirke White, 'Written

in the Prospect of Death'. This appears in *The poetical works of Henry Kirke White*, London: Bell and Daldy, 1830, p. 79. In this edition the lines read:

> – We have now
> But a small portion of what men call time
> To hold communion;

20. (p. 50). This is perhaps the passage in *Our Nig* that best of all illustrates Wilson's artistic restraint. Mrs. B.'s hypocritical recovery of strength is described: one minute too weak to help lift her invalid son, the next beating Frado so vigorously that she can be overheard. This incident invites sentimental over-emphasis. Yet the text resolutely declines to do this, to telling effect. The concision and matter-of fact tone that prevail enables the cruel silencing of Frado to be represented all the more damningly.

Chapter X

21. (p. 55). I have been so far unable to identify G. W. Cook with any conviction; the best bet seems to be George W. Cook, a maritime doctor, who signed himself Gco. W. Cook in his book, *The Mariner's Physician and Surgeon; or a Guide to the Homeopathic Treatment of Those Diseases to Which Seamen Are Liable, Comprising the Treatment of Syphilitic Diseases, &c.,* New York: J. T. S. Smith, 1848. Given the topic of the three lines of verse quoted by Wilson, this attribution has a shred of plausibility.

Chapter XI

22. (p. 60). The prolific Charlotte Elliott is the probable author of the lines quoted here by Wilson. She commonly signed herself C. E. Standing against this attribution is the fact that the lines are lacking the usual consolatory note to be found in Elliott. However, Elliott also makes frequent use of anaphora, in a characteristic poetic mannerism in which two or more lines begin with the same word

(in this case, 'Love'); she also recurrently wove reference to Christ's sacrifice into her verse (see, for example, her *Hours of Sorrow*, 1836).

23. (p. 62) The original edition carries the name 'Henry' here. Presumably this is an error, surviving from a redrafting. Henry has not appeared since Chapter V. Naming him here makes no sense; presumably 'Lewis' is intended?

Chapter XII

24. (p. 68). The slight misquote is taken from Ecclesiastes, 1, ix: 'The thing that hath been, it is that which shall be; and that which is done is that which shall be done: and there is no new thing under the sun.' A disturbing reflection, given the themes of this novel.

25. (p. 68). The strange phrase 'professed fugitives' ushers in a series of disturbances in this final chapter that successively complicate any Manichean representation of the contemporary debates concerning slavery. Here, the word 'professed' alerts one to the fact that in Northern US society, which had by 1859 come on balance to favour abolition, potential now existed for a new set of hypocrisies and oppressions to take root, as individuals exploited the growing anti-slavery consensus by trading on the money to be gained in this good cause. The following five footnotes explore these reverberations.

26. (p. 68). A reference to pro-slavery whites; the use of the term 'Brother' here is disturbing.

27. (p. 69). Samuel, Frado's husband, thus stands revealed as one of the 'professed fugitives' referred to on p. 68. Plainly, Samuel is exploiting the dominant ideological climate in the North. 'Humbug' is described as a '*low*' word in Webster's seventh edition. It is unclear whether the meaning of the word 'humbug' as 'sweetmeat' was in general circulation in America by 1859. The *OED* notes the first usage of this sense of the word 'humbug' occurs in 1825. If Wilson was intending a pun here, then it is a clever one, for it suggests that abolitionist lecture-circuit rhetoric is like 'sweets' for lecture audiences, rather than representing anything more meaty and sustaining.

28. (p. 69). This mention of 'kidnappers' seems most probably to be another reference to the consequences of the Fugitive Slave Act of 1850, which effectively gave licence to unscrupulous slave hunters to try to lay hands on any African Americans they encountered under the pretence that they were simply mistaking them for runaways (the Fugitive Slave Act allowed escaped slaves anywhere in the Union to be legitimately recaptured for return to the South). This danger of kidnap is here twinned with another danger: that of being 'maltreated by professed abolitionists'. Perhaps the most deadly and loaded phrase in the novel, this lays down the charge that racism is a deep-rooted problem in the North, infecting even the behaviour of supposed abolitionists. Thus George's earlier claim that 'thousands upon thousands favored the elevation of her race, disapproving of oppression in all its forms' (p. 40) is substantially undercut by Frado's quite different verdict upon abolitionist hypocrisy.

29. (p. 70). This bitter outburst by Wilson harshly illuminates the severity of some Northern abolitionists' racism.

30. (p. 70). 'Traps slyly laid by the vicious to ensnare her'. By now the reader is unsure whether this mention of 'traps' is another reference to the consequences of the Fugitive Slave Act of 1850, or a comment on the dangers created by Northern hypocrisy, or (most probably) both.

31. (p. 70). The reference is to Genesis 40, xxii, in which Pharaoh's butler fails to remember his promise to Joseph, to 'shew kindness unto' him (Genesis 40, xiv): 'Yet did not the chief butler remember Joseph, but forgat him.' It is striking that the three clear and direct references to biblical sources in the body of Wilson's novel (see also note 18 and note 24) are either to the Old Testament or, when to the New Testament, a reference laced with irony. This lends weight to my contention that Frado rests uneasy within her incomplete 'conversion narrative' (see note 37), particularly since the Appendix is, in contrast, stuffed full of biblical allusions, mostly to the New Testament (and not excepting Frado's own 'letter'. See also note 32).

Appendix

32. (p. 71). The Appendix consists of three testimonials. None of the testimonials' three authors has so far been identified. It is possible that they were written by Wilson herself, for there are some stylistic congruences between them and the preface, which is initialled as her own by Wilson (see my introduction). The first testimonial is signed by 'ALLIDA'. If she did exist, then she was most likely to be a worthy citizen of Milford, New Hampshire or its environs. The other two testimonial writers are named as MARGARETTA THORN and C. D. S. Nothing is know about either of these, in turn, but it is quite likely they were also simply worthy citizens of Milford, if they ever existed. It has been suggested that C. D. S. stands for 'Colored Indentured Servant', since C. D. S. was then a usual legal abbreviation. This idea lends force to the suggestion that these names are all pseudonyms used by Wilson in order to gain the authority bestowed by appending testimonials guaranteeing authenticity – a generic convention of slave narratives of that time.

33. (p. 71). Psalms, 23, v: 'thou anointest my head with oil: my cup runneth over.' This psalm is famous; particularly verse iv ('Yea though I walk through the valley of the shadow of death, I will fear no evil: for thou art with me; thy rod and thy staff they comfort me.'). Later in this same testimonial Allida quotes from the same psalm as Frado (see note 36), which may provide one further piece of evidence to support the claim I make in my introduction about Wilson's possible authorship of these testimonials (see note 32). The phrase 'what shall I render to the Lord for all his benefits' refers to Matthew 22, xxi: 'Render therefore unto Caesar the things which are Caesar's; and unto God the things that are God's.' This verse has been the site of constant theological controversy and was (mis)quoted by both pro-slavery and anti-slavery campaigners in support of their arguments. Its use here invests Alfrado's text in further ironies. See also Isaac Watts: 'What shall I render to my God/ For all his gifts to me?', 'Praise for Mercies, Spiritual and Temporal', in *The Works of the Reverend and*

Learned Isaac Watts ... Containing besides his Sermons and Essays on miscellaneous subjects, several additional pieces, Selected fom his Manuscripts by the Rev. Dr. Jennings and the Rev. Dr. Doldridge, in 1753: To which are prefixed memories of the life of the author, compiled by the Rev. George Burder, 6 vols., London: Printed by and for John Barfield [etc.], 1810, vol. 4, p. 394.

34. (p. 71). Jeremiah 10, xxiii: 'O LORD, I know that the way of man is not in himself: it is not in man that walketh to direct his steps.'

35. (p. 72). James 2, v: 'Hath not God chosen the poor of this world rich in faith, and heirs of the kingdom which he hath promised to them that love him?'

36. (p. 72). Psalms, 23, i: 'THE LORD is my shepherd; I shall not want.'

37. (p. 73). Psalm 40, xvii.

38. (p. 74). These verses do seem most likely not to have been plagiarised but to have been written by 'Alfrado'. Their unambiguously Christian sentiments stand as something of a contrast to Frado's more dubious and (at best) semi-consummated conversion to Christianity in the novel itself. Whilst it is true that the final chapter sees Frado 'reposing on God' (p. 70), this 'devout and Christian exterior' (p. 67) seems to be covering up doubts about whether Christianity was 'all for white people' (p. 45). The switch of tone present now, in these verses' unrelenting piousness, can, of course, be viewed ironically: as a strategic move, designed to persuade Wilson's readers of her merits as a charitable case. See also note 43, below.

39. (p. 74). Luke 14, xiv: 'for thou shalt be recompensed at the resurrection of the just.'

40. (p. 75). Isaiah 41, xiv.

41. (p. 76). It is unclear whether these verses are being presented as being written by 'ALLIDA' or as being quoted by her. If the latter, then the 'source' would be a hymn. However, the first four stanzas are composed in long measure and the last three in common measure. No hymn would make this sort of switch in its middle. It seems probable, therefore, that 'ALLIDA' or, more likely, Wilson

(if she really did write these testimonials – see note 32) is offering a pastiche here. Much of the phrasing in this poem is reminiscent of that of John and Charles Wesley. For example, the phrase 'supplicating cry' appears three times in *The poetical works of John and Charles Wesley: reprinted from the originals, with the last corrections of the authors; together with the poems of Charles Wesley not before published. Collected and arranged by G. Osborn*, 13 vols.; London: The Wesleyan Methodist Conference Office, 1868. Similarly, the phrasing of William Cowper and Isaac Watts are echoed in the first two stanzas. Compare these to the opening verse of Cowper's 'XXXVI. Light Shining Out of Darkness': 'God moves in a mysterious way/ His wonders to perform;/ He plants his footsteps in the sea,/ And rides upon the storm.', *The Works of William Cowper: Comprising his poems, correspondence, and translations. With a life of the author, by the editor, Robert Southey*, 15 vols.; London: Baldwin and Cradock, 1835 1837, vol. 8, p. 82. Compare them also to the opening verse of Watts: 'Our God, our help in ages past/ Our hope for years to come,/ Our shelter from the stormy blast,/ And our eternal home', 'Psalm xc', in *The Works of the Reverend and Learned Isaac Watts ... Containing besides his Sermons and Essays on miscellaneous subjects, several additional pieces, Selected fom his Manuscripts by the Rev. Dr. Jennings and the Rev. Dr. Doldridge, in 1753: To which are prefixed memories of the life of the author, compiled by the Rev. George Burder*, 6 vols., London: Printed by and for John Barfield [etc.], 1810, vol. 4, p.191.

42. (p. 76). See note 32.

43. (p. 77). The patronisingly sententious tone of this nostrum reminds one forcibly of Charles Kingsley, whose *The Water Babies* was to be published in 1863 (shortly after *Our Nig*). Many examples of this sort of sanctimoniousness lurk in mid-Nineteenth Century writing. If, as I suggest, this testimonial is actually the work of Wilson, then there are resonant ironies present in the Franklinesque tone of MARGARETTA THORN's writing ('Therefore we should do with all our might what our hands find to do ... . Therefore, let us work while the day lasts, and we shall in no wise lose our reward', p. 78).

It is, perhaps, reasonable to suggest that this sort of unreflective sententiousness is, precisely, a 'THORN' in the side of Frado, and therefore a sign of Wilson's strategies in appending these testimonials (see note 32 and my introduction).

44. (p. 78). Matthew 25, xl: 'Inasmuch as ye have done it unto one of the least of these my brethren, ye have done it unto me.'

45. (p. 78). See note 32.

46. (p. 78). 'MILFORD': it was this single word at the head of C. D. S.'s testimonial that enabled Henry Louis Gates Jr and, subsequently, Barbara A. White to track down the historical identity of Harriet Wilson.

47. (p. 78). See note 32.

Modernisations to the 1859 text of *Our Nig*.

The following notes are of two sorts. The original edition of *Our Nig* was printed somewhat carelessly. This carelessness probably indicates that the novel's printing was carried out as cheaply as possible by Rand & Avery. One reason why this might in turn be the case is that George Curtis Rand was an abolitionist sympathiser, and so was carrying out the printing in part (or even wholly) as a charitable endeavour (see Gardner, 1993, p. 226). The first edition therefore contains many errors or irregularities. Other errors may derive from the fact that this printing firm did not usually handle novels, and may therefore have been unfamiliar with the conventions that existed. The resulting errors and irregularities have been silently amended in this edition, and these amendments are noted below.

The bulk of the notes, however, indicate where, in the original edition, words were printed with a space (either an en-space or, more usually, an em-space) introduced where more contemporary usage would print the word with no such space. The decision was made to alter these words because the original 1859 edition of *Our Nig* repeatedly used both versions of almost all of the words, interchangeably. To give just one example of this: on p. 4 l. 23 the sentence originally appeared as "'She'd be as much a prize to me as she 'd fall short of coming up to the mark with white folks.'" In the present edition, this is regularised, and so is reprinted as "'She'd be as much a prize to me as she'd fall short of coming up to the mark with white folks.'" The fact that two versions of the same word appear in the same sentence well illustrates how the introduction of a space in mid-word exists without any pattern in the original edition.

PAGE	LINE	
3	20	'don't' appeared as 'do n't'.
3	23	'don't' appeared as 'do n't'.
3	27	'isn't' appeared as 'is n't'.
4	8	'Don't' appeared as 'Do n't'.
4	24	'she'd' appeared as 'she 'd'.
4	25	'don't' appeared as 'do n't'.
4	26	'She's' appeared as 'She 's'.
4	30	'How's' appeared as 'How 's'.
5	3	'you's' appeared as 'you 's'.
5	4	'don't' appeared as 'do n't'.
7	8	'insurmountable' appeared as 'iusurmountable'.
7	22	'It's' appeared as 'It 's
7	24	'Who'll' appeared as 'Who 'll'.
7	25	'They're' appeared as 'They 're'.
7	27	'We'll' appeared as 'We 'll'.
7	27	'There's' appeared as 'There 's.
7	27	'Frado's' appeared as 'Frado 's'.
7	28	'folks'll' appeared as 'folks 'll'.
7	28	'She'd' appeared as 'She 'd'.
8	3	'Wouldn't' appeared as 'Would n't'.
8	5	'Hadn't' appeared as 'Had n't'.
8	10	'she's' appeared as 'she 's'.
8	11	'we've' appeared as 'we 've'.
8	14	'One's' appeared as 'One 's'.
8	14	't'other' appeared as 't' other'.
8	15	'she's' appeared as 'she 's'.

PAGE	LINE	
8	15	'wo n't' appeared as 'wo n't'.
8	16	'don't' appeared as 'do n't' on both occasions.
8	21	'We're' appeared as 'We 're'.
8	26	'She's' appeared as 'She 's'.
8	26	'I'd' appeared as 'I 'd'.
10	4	'decrepit' appeared as 'decrepid'. The latter spelling is described as 'erroneous' in Webster's seventh (abridged) edition, 1856.
11	14	'sympathy' appeared as 'symathy'.
12	6	'She's' appeared as 'She 's'.
12	8	'that's' appeared as 'that 's'.
12	8	'She'll' appeared as 'She 'll'.
12	10	'wouldn't' appeared as 'would n't'.
12	12	'don't' appeared as 'do n't'.
12	13	'don't' appeared as 'do n't'.
12	19	'don't' appeared as 'do n't'.
12	21	'How'll' appeared as 'How 'll'.
12	23	'She'll' appeared as 'She 'll'.
12	23	'it's' appeared as 'it 's'.
13	12	'didn't' appeared as 'did n't'.
16	18	'didn't' appeared as 'did n't' on both occasions.
16	33	'can't' appeared as 'can 't'.
21	24	'protegé' was the contemporary spelling of 'protégé', according to Webster's seventh edition (1856)
22	16	'Aunt' appeared as 'Anut'.
23	15	'ha'n't' appeared as 'ha' n't'.
23	27	'Where's' appeared as 'Where 's'.
24	3	Mrs. B. appeared as 'Mrs, B.'.
24	20	'There comes': sic.
24	28	'What's' appeared as 'What 's'.
24	31	'What's' appeared as 'What 's'.
24	29	'She's' appeared as 'She 's'.
24	34	'shan't' appeared as 'shan 't'.

PAGE	LINE	
25	8	'I'll' appeared as 'I 'll'.
28	11	The word is spelt 'willful' in the original edition both on this line and 13 lines later, a spelling endorsed by Webster's seventh.
28	18	'Mr.' appeared as 'Mr' (with no full stop).
29	17	The word is spelt 'incumbrance' in the original edition.
30	23	'don't' appeared as 'do n't'.
30	25	'won't' appeared as 'wo n't'.
31	20	'Don't' appeared as 'Do n't'.
33	12	'housekeeper' appeared as 'housekeper'.
34	8	'done?' appeared as 'done' (with no punctuation).
34	29	'I'll' appeared as 'I 'll'.
35	11	The word 'illy' appeared in the original edition. Webster's seventh edition notes: 'A word sometimes used, though improperly, for *ill.*'
35	15	'incessant' appeared as 'inccessant'.
35	20	'apartment' appeared as 'appartment'.
36	10	The quotation marks are omitted in the original: 'imperatively; "I'm ..."' appeared as 'imperatively; I'm ..."'.
38	13	''twas' appeared as ''t was'.
39	22	'the world are': sic.
40	9	'can't' appeared as 'can 't'.
40	32	'don't' appeared as 'do n't'.
43	4	'delinquencies' appeared as 'delinquinces'.
43	13	'She's' appeared as 'She 's'.
43	13	'she's' appeared as 'she 's'.
43	16	'she's' appeared as 'she 's'.
43	16	'she'll' appeared as 'she 'll'.
43	18	'that's' appeared as 'that 's'.
43	20	'she'll' appeared as 'she 'll'.
43	21	'wouldn't' appeared as 'would n't'.

PAGE	LINE	
43	23	'I'd' appeared as 'I 'd'.
43	27	'Didn't' appeared as 'Did n't'.
47	27	'wasn't' appeared as 'was n't'.
48	2	'Don't' appeared as 'Do n't'.
48	15	'can't' appeared as 'ca n't'.
56	2	The quotation marks are omitted in the original: "'Why, aunt, ...'" appeared as 'Why, aunt ...'".
50	2	'What' appeared as 'W at'.
50	9	The word 'not' was erroneously omitted: 'he did not want' appeared as 'he did want'.
53	21	'Aunt Abby' appeared as 'aunt Abby'.
54	20	'upbraided' appeared as 'upraided'.
57	29	'pop in into': sic.
57	30	'didn't' appeared as 'did n't'.
57	31	'she'll' appeared as 'she 'll'.
57	32	'Wouldn't' appeared as 'Would n't'.
60	16	'for," asked': sic; comma used instead of question mark.
60	18	'she's' appeared as 'she 's'.
60	20	'family for' appeared as 'family, for'.
60	21	'couldn't' appeared as 'could n't'.
62	24	'wouldn't' appeared as 'would n't'.
63	13	'mustn't' appeared as 'must n't'.
64	9	'succor could': sic; comma omitted.
65	1	'You're' appeared as 'You 're'.
65	2	'she'll' appeared as 'she 'll'.
65	8	'shan't' appeared as 'sha n't'.
65	30	"'she shall never ... '" appeared as "'she she shall never ... '".
69	32	'didn't' appeared as 'did n't'.
72	29	Punctuation omitted: 'want.' appeared as 'want' in the original.
77	29	'these words, Do good': sic; the quote which follows is not placed in quotation marks.